The Complete Guide to Planning Your Estate In Virginia:

A Step-By-Step Plan to Protect Your Assets, Limit Your Taxes, and Ensure Your Wishes Are Fulfilled for Virginia Residents

By Linda C. Ashar, J.D., and Sandy Baker

THE COMPLETE GUIDE TO PLANNING YOUR ESTATE IN VIRGINIA: A STEP-BY-STEP PLAN TO PROTECT YOUR ASSETS, LIMIT YOUR TAXES, AND ENSURE YOUR WISHES ARE FULFILLED FOR VIRGINIA RESIDENTS

1405 SW 6th Avenue • Ocala, Florida 34471 • Phone 800-814-1132 • Fax 352-622-1875
Web site: www.atlantic-pub.com • E-mail: sales@atlantic-pub.com
SAN Number: 268-1250

Library of Congress Cataloging-in-Publication Data

Ashar, Linda C., 1947-
The complete guide to planning your estate in Virginia : a step-by-step plan to protect your assets, limit your taxes, and ensure your wishes are fulfilled for Virginia residents / by Linda C. Ashar and Sandy Baker.
p. cm.
Includes bibliographical references and index.
ISBN-13: 978-1-60138-436-2 (alk. paper)
ISBN-10: 1-60138-436-X (alk. paper)
1. Estate planning--Virginia--Popular works. I. Baker, Sandy Ann, 1976- II. Title.
KFV2540.A974 2009
346.75505'2--dc22

2009045275

Printed in the United States

PROJECT MANAGER: Melissa Peterson • mpeterson@atlantic-pub.com
INTERIOR DESIGN: Samantha Martin • smartin@atlantic-pub.com
ASSISTANT EDITOR: Angela Pham • apham@atlantic-pub.com
COVER AND JACKET DESIGN: Jackie Miller • sullmill@charter.net

Printed on Recycled Paper

We recently lost our beloved pet "Bear," who was not only our best and dearest friend but also the "Vice President of Sunshine" here at Atlantic Publishing. He did not receive a salary but worked tirelessly 24 hours a day to please his parents. Bear was a rescue dog that turned around and showered myself, my wife, Sherri, his grandparents Jean, Bob, and Nancy, and every person and animal he met (maybe not rabbits) with friendship and love. He made a lot of people smile every day.

We wanted you to know that a portion of the profits of this book will be donated to The Humane Society of the United States. ***–Douglas & Sherri Brown***

The human-animal bond is as old as human history. We cherish our animal companions for their unconditional affection and acceptance. We feel a thrill when we glimpse wild creatures in their natural habitat or in our own backyard.

Unfortunately, the human-animal bond has at times been weakened. Humans have exploited some animal species to the point of extinction.

The Humane Society of the United States makes a difference in the lives of animals here at home and worldwide. The HSUS is dedicated to creating a world where our relationship with animals is guided by compassion. We seek a truly humane society in which animals are respected for their intrinsic value, and where the human-animal bond is strong.

Want to help animals? We have plenty of suggestions. Adopt a pet from a local shelter, join The Humane Society and be a part of our work to help companion animals and wildlife. You will be funding our educational, legislative, investigative and outreach projects in the U.S. and across the globe.

Or perhaps you'd like to make a memorial donation in honor of a pet, friend or relative? You can through our Kindred Spirits program. And if you'd like to contribute in a more structured way, our Planned Giving Office has suggestions about estate planning, annuities, and even gifts of stock that avoid capital gains taxes.

Maybe you have land that you would like to preserve as a lasting habitat for wildlife. Our Wildlife Land Trust can help you. Perhaps the land you want to share is a backyard—that's enough. Our Urban Wildlife Sanctuary Program will show you how to create a habitat for your wild neighbors.

So you see, it's easy to help animals. And The HSUS is here to help.

THE HUMANE SOCIETY OF THE UNITED STATES.

2100 L Street NW • Washington, DC 20037 • 202-452-1100

www.hsus.org

Trademark Statement

Virginia Facts

In Virginia, a person age 18 or older is of legal age to make a will, unless emancipated at a younger age.

In Virginia, you may write your will out by hand, type it, or print it out from your computer.

You must name a person to be the executor (referred to in Virginia as "personal representative") who will administer your will.

Virginia law does not recognize nuncupative wills.

In Virginia, a will provision granting anything to a spouse is automatically revoked once the marriage is divorced, dissolved, or annulled.

Virginia provides for homestead and family allowance.

Virginia recognizes a "holographic" will, that is, a document made entirely in your own handwriting and signed.

Virginia law prescribes a method for depositing your will during your lifetime with the clerk of court in the county in which you reside.

Dedication

"To my husband and children, who have helped me to create the life I've dreamed of living." – Sandy Baker

"To my mother, who has steadfastly encouraged me in all things." – Linda C. Ashar, J.D.

Table of Contents

Chapter 2: What Are You Worth? 41

Chapter 3: Your Will: The Definition of Your Estate Plan 55

Colonial Windmill, Williamsburg, Virginia

Foreword

Just mentioning the need for an estate plan often throws people into an instant state of guilt over not having one and confusion about how to start. What information is required? Which professionals should be contacted? What decisions need to be made? For most people, it is just easier to put it off — again. Throughout my 18 years of practicing estate planning law, I constantly compared the ease of administering a clear estate plan to the turmoil caused when a family member died without a plan. One of the best gifts, and certainly the last gift, a person leaves his or her family is a well-planned estate.

It is never too early to start thinking about an estate plan. The sooner a plan is started, the more options are available to the client. For example, life insurance frequently is an important component of a good plan, and policies are cheaper at a younger age. Starting relatively early in life usually means there is less financial information to organize, and updating becomes a lifelong habit. Moreover, clearly stating health care wishes and appointing a person to direct them are important at every age because accidents happen. The trauma of an accident is exacerbated when sensitive health care decisions must be made on assumptions, leaving family members, doctors, or even judges guessing about the patient's values.

The Complete Guide to Planning Your Estate in Virginia is the perfect companion in the planning process. It explains the information needed to start — what assets are included in the estate, the effect of debt, who can help — and how to obtain that information. The terminology and options involved with probate, trusts, insurance, and the estate tax can be overwhelming. In my experience, many clients leave their first meeting with a professional feeling dazed. With *The Complete Guide to Planning Your Estate in Virginia*, clients can enter the meeting with an understanding of the process and know they have a resource to refer to every step along the way.

Estate planning is a combination of federal tax law and state administration law. Any guide must include the fundamentals of the tax provisions and property transfer options, but also the particular rules specific to each state. Not following the state laws can cause delay and additional fees to correct mistakes, or worse, could invalidate portions of a plan. This guide is designed to inform Virginia residents of their options and the rules for implementing their plans.

Recently, Stieg Larsson, the bestselling Swedish author, wrote all three books of the Millennium trilogy and died of a heart attack before any were published. They are a huge hit, resulting in millions of kroners in Larsson's estate. Who receives the money? He lived with a woman for years; she was his life companion, but they never married. He did have a will prepared years ago giving the money to an organization, but he never signed it. As in Virginia, Sweden has intestate laws that decide who receives a deceased person's assets in the event there is not a will. Under these laws, Larsson's father and brother are very wealthy men.

If you do not have an estate plan, get started.

Kim L. Allen-Niesen

Kim L. Allen-Niesen practiced estate planning law for 18 years. She attended Boalt Hall School of Law, University of California, Berkeley, and then practiced estate planning for several years in large law firms in Los Angeles before opening her own practice. Allen-Niesen owned her own practice for 12 years and retired in 2007.

Governors Mansion, Williamsburg, Virginia

Introduction

Your estate is what you have worked to develop over your lifetime. You deserve to make decisions about the distribution of your property and your money.

Using this book as a guide, with its easy-to-understand language, you will learn how to plan your estate legally.

With a will in hand and a plan for your estate, you can be assured that your wishes will be met and that you have taken the steps to:

- Protect your loved ones from taxes that can literally take most of your estate.
- Give your favorite charities the funds you want them to have.
- Save your survivors from making decisions about your estate.
- Provide for your loved ones.

An estimated 60 percent of people die without a will or any type of estate plan. That means that the government settles the estate, and, if there are no clearly defined heirs, the state takes everything.

Your estate plan is a living document that changes with you. As your life moves forward, your estate plan can provide for life changes. By getting your wishes down on paper now, you take care of everyone who is important to you, no matter what happens, so that they have the funds they need to live without you.

This simple, easy-to-follow book will help you to understand each step of the estate process and allow you to protect those you love.

Chapter 1

An Introduction to Estate Planning

Why Do All This Work?

If you want to decide what happens to your money and possessions, you need to do it through your estate plan.

When you do plan your estate, you can do several important things:

1. Because of a rising divorce rate and people's choices of lifestyle, the normal family today may include numbers of people whom the law will not take into consideration when examining who will be covered by your estate plan.

2. You cut or eliminate the amount the government takes from your estate in the form of taxes, fees, and costs.

3. You protect your business. An estate plan can help the business stay open and thriving with structured succession planning.

CASE STUDY: JANICE ENGELBERTH

Warsaw, IN

What is the most important thing for others to consider, based on your experience, when it comes to planning an estate?

Learn about the taxes that are due for the estate and when they are due.

My husband's health did not allow him to sign documents, and even though I had the power of attorney, I could not sign his name on real estate documents. I made sure there was one bank account with the minimum amount kept in it for cashing government checks, and I found that process to be a challenge, too.

If one is able, prepay funeral expenses so that this burden does not happen later.

I also found that it was important to make sure that all people involved have a medical directive, as this could be a potential problem when something happens. We established all these things in an effort to make the process after death easier.

When you completed the process, did you feel secure?

Yes, I did feel like I was in a better place for whatever comes. It was worth the effort to know that everything was planned. We worked through a lawyer who specialized in trusts. Before, we had almost all our holdings in joint ownership accounts. In 2000, each of us had a trust. In 2006, it was revised because of health issues. We wanted to sell real estate, and he could not write his name to sign the documents. If we did not have the trust, our four children would have had to sell property quickly to pay the almost $250,000 in taxes that would be due.

What is an Estate?

Often, people think they do not have enough of an estate to have to worry about planning. But if you have a home, other assets, credit card debt, or heirs, you need to plan your estate. Your estate consists of everything that belongs to you. Here are some items that come into play when planning your estate:

- Actual money: This includes cash that you may have, as well as checking and savings accounts.
- Certificates of deposit.
- Your investment portfolio: Stocks, mutual funds, and bonds.
- Your retirement funds: Pension funds, 401(k), IRAs, and any other money that has been reserved for retirement.
- Profit-sharing funds with employer.
- Your house, vehicles, boats, equipment, livestock, and all property inside your home, including clothing, furniture, appliances, your jewelry, and other valuables.
- Insurance products: Life insurance, especially.
- Your business: Any funds or ownership interest of your business.
- Annuities that you may have coming to you.
- Anything else that you have that you consider valuable, either sentimentally or monetarily.

One important note is that your estate planning will likely include both positive and negative balance amounts. For example, it will include all the items listed above as positive balances, provided they do not carry a loan or a negative balance. A mortgage on your home or other real estate you own is a negative amount because it means you owe money on it. Principal equity in the property, though, is a positive. In addition to these things, money you owe others, taxes you owe, and any credit you have outstanding are also a negative balance against your assets.

Even though assets may carry a negative balance against them in debt, they still factor into your estate plan. It is essential to know this information to figure out your estate's actual worth and to plan how its worth can increase.

What is your estate worth?

It is simple math to figure out what your estate is worth. Start by adding all the positive items together for the value of your assets. For items such as jewelry, coin collections, other collectibles, and antiques, you may need appraisals if you cannot place a value yourself with reasonable accuracy.

Next, subtract the amount of money that you owe from this asset balance. The balance is the net value of your assets.

If you own a business, for example, you will need to know the value of the business itself, all equipment, and the value of your stock.

Any money or property that you reasonably expect will be yours in the future may need to be included in your estate as well.

Remember: The value of your estate will change over time.

Property Types

There are several different types of property that should be included in your estate. The most common is that of real property, including any type of real estate that you might own, such as a timeshare, and any improvements you have made to the land you own.

Personal property is broken down into two types: tangible and intangible. Tangible personal property is any type of property that can be physically touched. Examples are clothing, jewelry, and furniture.

Intangible personal property includes money, bank accounts, investment accounts, and stock certificates. It includes anything that is financially oriented that belongs to you.

Property Interest: Defined

The two types of property interest include legal interest and beneficial interest.

Legal interest means that you only have a legal right to the property, but you do not have the ability to use it. One example is a trust. If you are the trustee of property that belongs to someone else, you get to make decisions about how that property is used, but you do not get to use those funds or property for your own benefit. As trustee, you make decisions about the money but cannot touch the funds for your own use.

The second type of property interest is beneficial interest. Here, you do have the benefit from the property, meaning that you do have use of and the right to the property. There are two additional types of interest that are defined as beneficial:

- **Present interest**: In this type of interest, you have the right to use the interest right now, as you see fit. Here, there is no wait to get the benefits from your property.

- **Future interest**: As the name describes, you have the benefit coming to you in the future. This type of interest can be further broken down:

  - **Vested interest** is the benefit that you get in future interest that allows you to do anything you want with no strings attached.

  - **Contingent interest** is the benefit that you will get only if you abide by the rules set forth.

Who Will Help You Plan Your Estate?

While you could do all your estate planning yourself, it is better to use some key people along the way to help you to make the most of estate planning and avoid potential pitfalls, whether legal or your own oversight. Each one plays their own role in helping you to get your estate set up with a plan for its future.

You should utilize the services of four key individuals during this process.

- **Legal counsel**: You will need a good estate planning attorney. Having someone whose specialty is estate planning makes the best sense. Virginia does not certify specialists in the law, but you can research lawyers who have an experienced track record in estate planning and probate.

- **Accountant**: Next, you need an accountant to help you determine value and manage taxes on your estate, one who can help you make the right decisions now to avoid costly taxes later on.

- **Financial planner**: A financial planner who can assist you in making decisions regarding investments and other finances will also be needed. You may consult with a financial planner for guidance only, or turn over investment and management of your estate. In the latter case, be very careful of whom you select. Get references from your legal counsel and accountant, and utilize someone who can demonstrate an established track record to support this person's trustworthiness.

- **Insurance agent**: Finally, you need the help of an insurance agent to explore this form of protection for family and assets. The obvious benefit here is life insurance, but you should also consider disability insurance as well as liability insurance and coverage for home and assets against fire, theft, and other disasters.

A Closer Look: The Attorney

An attorney should be able to look at your situation and prepare for possible scenarios. What if you die before you get married but you still want all your belongings to go to your fiancé? What if your heir dies before you do? All these (and countless more) situations are something that your attorney needs to plan out for you.

Ask your attorney to provide you with the legal advice necessary in handling trusts, wills, your business, and every aspect of your estate planning.

What to look for in an attorney

You should look for these qualities in the attorney you retain:

- *Look for an attorney who specializes in estate planning.* What experience does he or she have that will serve your needs? Ask about the person's legal experience in your area and with people whose financial situation is similar to yours. What amount of dedication and time can your attorney give you?

- *Can you trust the attorney?* You want someone who you feel has your best interests at heart and who is working for you. You also should like the person, as you will be dealing with him or her for some time to come.

A Closer Look: The Financial Planner

The financial planner has the job of helping you make your financial dreams come true and to give you the advice that you need to manage your funds over the course of your lifetime. With a financial planner, you will be able to provide for your loved ones when you are gone.

It is important to determine the role of your planner. Some people want to find someone they can trust, pay a fixed amount of money per month to manage investments, and watch their numbers rise. Others want only to be told how to handle their funds, such as which investments are good choices, and then make the final decisions themselves. You could be someplace in the middle.

What to look for in a financial planner

For most people, it is important to take into consideration whom they will be working with. You need to find someone you can trust; someone you know has your best interests at heart. To do that, ask these questions when searching for a financial planner:

- *What is the person/firm's background?* What credentials do they have that will fit with what you need and want from them? You want to know this and how it relates to what you need.

- *What do they do?* One thing that is essential to take note of is the fact that financial planners are all different. It is recommended you choose a Certified Financial Planner® (CFP®), as he or she must pass an exam to become licensed. This follows a long list of financial training courses at the college level. In addition, the financial planner needs to have at least three years of experience working with financial planning clients. While there are many other types of financial planners out there, you want one who has the title to go along with the skills.

- *How is the financial planner paid?* It is important to determine this for the financial planners you are considering. Those who get a commission from the products that they say you must have are not the best choice. There is an inherent conflict of interest in such an arrangement. Look for those who are paid a fee only, or those who are paid based on how well your portfolio does. Make sure you clearly understand whether the financial planner is getting paid to sell you a product.

CASE STUDY: WILLIAM RUSSO, CFP

Certified Financial Planner
33595 Bainbridge Road, Suite 104
Solon, Ohio, 44139
Phone: (440) 349-4980
E-mail: Brusso@concordfinancialplan.com
Web Address: **www.concordfinancialplan.com**

In consideration of the timeliness of starting estate planning, the best time is now. Each time you title an account or designate a beneficiary, you are estate planning. Each person/couple needs to evaluate their current situation, and consider how they would want their estate to be distributed if something were to happen to them. If their children are under 18, do they want the executor and guardian to make decisions as to how and when their children get access to their estate? These decisions need to be made now, not at a later date; nobody knows what tomorrow brings.

Baby boomers need to make sure that their retirement assets are set up in a way that their heirs have tax-favorable access to the retirement accounts. This means knowing whether it is better to leave assets in company plans, or roll them over to IRAs. Planning now ensures that if something were to happen to you, your heirs would be taken care of with the estate while minimizing tax exposure.

The job of the financial planner is to make people take the time to identify their goals, educate them as to the options available, and make sure that their recommendations are followed through on. Once a plan is implemented, then

CASE STUDY: WILLIAM RUSSO, CFP

ongoing review ensures that the plan is modified to take into account changes that occur.

A person should expect to spend an hour to an hour-and-a-half discussing their current situations (net worth, spending plan), goals and priorities, time frames, and what is important to them and why. What got them to this point, what has worked, what has not, what other professionals they work with, and what outcomes they desire to make them feel the relationship is worthwhile all will be discussed.

My job can only be successful if there is a level of trust, and all information that affects their financial affairs is disclosed. This is mutual, as I must be able to convey a level of trust before anyone would feel comfortable disclosing their financial affairs, thoughts, and concerns.

A financial planner is a good investment because they are an independent entity who can provide objective insight into a person's financial affairs. A planner should never tell a client what they want to hear, but should explain to them the impact of decisions that are made on their financial plan. We try to make sure people understand that to build wealth, they must first spend less than they earn. We see to it that clients commit to and follow a sound, long-term investment strategy. We reinforce the need to stay disciplined and exercise patience.

A Closer Look: The Accountant

The accountant is a key player on your estate planning team, and you should ensure that he or she has what it takes to provide you with the help you need. Your accountant's job is to help you to see how the tax side of estate planning will work. Think of the accountant who is hired for a business (maybe even your own). He or she has the job of helping the business to manage its money, to do its tax returns, and to advise where it stands at any one point. In addition, the accountant looks at the investments being made and helps with decisions regarding taxes in the future. He or she might tell you that if you invest X amount of dollars into upgrading equipment, you can claim it as a deduction. The same scenario is true for your accountant on the estate planning team you are building.

The accountant will work with you to determine where you stand right now, and where you are headed. He might suggest a few changes now so that, down the road, you can avoid some costly mistakes, or keep you on top of the latest changes in tax laws regarding your estate. One of the key things he does is advise how to give "financial gifts" so that they benefit you from a tax aspect.

What to look for in an accountant

The accountant plays a primary role, and therefore, you should have some clear-cut goals when it comes to choosing this advisor for estate planning. Here are some qualities to look for in a qualified accountant.

- *Is he or she a CPA?* You want to ensure that the accountant you select is a Certified Public Accountant. This means that he or she has taken the necessary educational steps toward earning a license from the American Institute of Certified Public Accountants — not an easy feat.

- *Who is the firm?* You should ensure that the accountant you hire is not working for anyone who may encourage him or her to sell you products that you do not necessarily need. You can easily learn this by simply asking.

- *What experience does the accountant have working in estate planning?* This is key because many CPAs will have a specialty field; just because they know how to do basic estate planning accounting does not necessarily mean they know all there is to know about it. You want someone who can provide you with a specialty in estate planning.

Taking the time necessary to find these traits can pay off right away. A good accountant can meet with you to discuss the changes needed to be made quickly and begin working on a strategy with you to improve your tax burden down the road. You will save money in the long-term by investing in an able accountant now.

A Closer Look: The Insurance Agent

The final piece to the puzzle of estate planning is your insurance agent. It is important to know just what this resource can offer you in regard to estate planning. We will go into more detail about life insurance and other insurance products, but for now, realize the importance of getting someone on-board to help with these decisions.

The difference with an insurance agent from the other three advisors is that he or she will be looking to sell you products. A good one will help you to wade through the different options until you find something that works for your particular needs. But some will also try to convince you to purchase things you do not need. What is most important is finding someone you can trust.

You should have an insurance agent on your estate planning team if you have any dependants, such as a spouse, children, or anyone who will need some protection and help when you die. The scope of this need will likely change over time. Insurance is like a blanket of protection that you can throw over your loved ones in times of trouble. While money cannot solve everything, it will help a family to survive a catastrophic event, such as premature death or severe disability.

What to look for in an insurance agent

You might already have an insurance agent handling your automobile insurance or your house insurance. If you like and trust these individuals, and their company offers the types of insurance that you need, then by all means, work with them.

- *What is their experience?* In the field of insurance agents, you need to find out what they can help you with when it comes to estate planning tools. They should offer a wide range of life insurance, disability insurance, and liability insurance products. They should also be willing and capable of helping you find a product that meets your needs.

- *Do you trust them?* You should find an insurance agent whom you can trust to explain and deliver a product that gives you the type of coverage you need. Sometimes, there is someone who has been in the family for years, and you want to use him or her. Do so, but only if he or she is a comparable choice to others out there. When you purchase a product, you need to know it is what you think it is. Your agent should make time for you, too, explaining every last detail that you do not understand.

- *Is what they are offering cost effective?* There is a range in price when it comes to insurance products. You might want to consider looking at several agents who fit into the above categories who can provide you with the best rate. This means looking at the short- and long-term of each of your goals.

Finding the right agent is a must for estate planning. The good news is that many are more than willing to help you.

Getting Started with Your Estate Planning

Now that you know what it means and what it takes to plan your estate, you can move into the process of making it happen.

There are many ways that you can do this, and you can even hire someone to do it all for you. Nevertheless, it is your job to see it through from beginning to end. The process itself is just that: a process. You cannot possibly get it all figured out in a heartbeat — it will take days, weeks, and even months to come to fruition. The good news is that the end result is well-worth the process that it takes to get there.

The normal process of setting up an estate plan is what you should be following. You need to invest time in making each step happen, and have a clearly defined plan. If you read this book and say, "I have to do these things," and never put your hand to it, then you will not realize your goals.

What makes it even more challenging to many is the fact that it takes time to work through each step. If you go to set up a trust and find that you need to fill out some additional paperwork, get some signatures, and then realize that there might be another route that is better, then you change paths, get frustrated, and eventually just do not move through the process. For this reason, you need to establish a resolve to complete the job.

Here, we will reveal a few things to put your mind to now, to get you started. In each chapter of this book, you will find the details that you need to bring together each step in the process.

Your Method for Success

Here is an example of the plan to get you from not having an estate plan to having one that completely fills your needs. Will you make it there? If you follow these steps, you are sure to make it to the summit.

Step 1: What are your goals?

You sat down with this book for a reason. It might be that you are trying to figure out how to help your elderly parents. Or you might be concerned about what could happen to your family if you were to die suddenly. Your goals are likely to be situated around these factors. No matter what your goals are, you should have them in mind while working on your estate planning.

What is it that you want to accomplish by having an estate plan in place?

- Protecting your spouse if you die?
- Helping your children pay for college?
- Helping to protect your home and investments?
- Making your wishes come true?
- Ensuring that you have the funds to manage a life that you want to live?

Take the time right now to stop reading and to write down your goals. This is something that you should take pencil and paper to, because when things get confusing during estate planning, you will be able to come back and say definitively, "This is what my goal is."

Step 2: Get your team situated

As we mentioned, it is important to have professionals working for you. Believe it or not, this step in the process might take you a few extra weeks to complete. To choose those who are best-suited for your needs, you should be comparing several. For example, if you are going to be looking for an insurance agent, talk to several and find out what they can offer you. Plan to meet with these individuals and get a feel for what they can do to serve your needs.

Eventually, you will want to select the person who has the best outlook for your lifestyle and needs, but also the one whom you seem to work the best with. If you do not like a person's personality, are you likely to call that person when you have a question?

Hiring people to help you plan your estate is one of the smartest decisions you can make. You want to find others who are willing to help you through the process, step by step, and are in it for the long-term.

Finally, make sure your team is working together. You want your attorney to be able to contact your accountant and let him or her know about a new plan that might be working. Likewise, your financial planner might suggest a new investment, but your accountant might be leery because of the tax implications that it has. Getting them to work together can be one of the best moves you make.

Step 3: Do your homework

As much as you did not like doing homework while you were in school, it is now more important than ever to have the information that you need to make the right decisions, and homework is the best way to do it.

Although you are hiring people to help you develop an estate plan, you are still the leader of the team, and therefore, you need to make sure that all the right moves are being made. To get started, learn where you stand right now and what you can do to improve to the position that you would like to be at. For example, you want to ensure that your financial investments are working for you right now, in the long- and short-term. You want to ensure that if you have a will, it is completely up-to-date on your current situation.

You should do your own research on the benefits of estate planning and which products are best for you. This book is one of the best tools that you have available to you. Keeping yourself educated about the options and new laws, taxes, and scandals that are out there helps you to keep yourself on the path to having an ideal estate plan.

Step 4: Develop and implement an action plan

Many times during business management courses, you will hear about the action plan. You might cringe at the number of times that you have had to write these, and you might have thought them to be ridiculous. But look back at the number of times that they have helped you. Now, implement this into your current life and your estate planning needs.

Develop a plan of how you will accomplish your goals. You will work on your will this week. Next week, you will meet with your financial planner to begin looking at investments that can be helpful to you down the road. The week after, you will meet with your accountant to talk about gifts that you can give that will help you with your taxes. You might schedule a time to work out the important qualifications of the trusts you want to set up. As you can see, there is quite a bit to do.

While this book will take you through much of this, you should implement these steps now. Read through this book; determine what your goals are and what you need to do; then, execute each step by going through the book a second time, this time moving forward only when you have made headway on what you are currently working on.

Your action plan should be something that motivates you, too. Think of the relief you will have knowing that your family is taken care of. Think of the benefits you will gain just by working with a financial planner to get your finances in order. If you feel the need, allow yourself a reward for accomplishing these important tasks.

Develop a plan of when you will work on your estate plan; how you will get the plan accomplished, including a time table for progress; and what you want to make happen. Enforce this by doing what you say you need to do.

Hold yourself accountable for the action plan, too. If you decide to work on the plan five hours per week, then do so. Although it sounds morbid, none of us knows whether we have another 60 years or two weeks to live. Dedicating time to complete your estate plan is necessary.

Step 5: Come back to it

The one mistake that many people make is that of planning out their estate, only to forget about it. Your estate is not something that will stay the same throughout the course of your life, nor will what you put into your plan remain the same. Because of these variables, you will need to come back and revisit the key issues of your estate plan to ensure that it provides you with the utmost protection and the clearest goals for how your life is being lived right now, not how it was.

Many people make a will and then just tuck it away and forget about it. When they die, their heirs are insulted because their ex-wife or their fourth unexpected child was not included in the will, or there might be additional property that does not get figured in because the will was not updated to include it. Each of these things can cause problems for you or your loved ones down the road.

The good news is that a good estate planning attorney should be willing to revisit your will yearly — including all your estate plans — and update as necessary. Perhaps every year around your birthday or another predetermined date, you want to plan some time to look over what is in place, and make decisions about it if needed.

This does not have to be a long, drawn-out process. Just picking up your will and looking at it is better than tucking it into a safety deposit box and forgetting about it. Life changes every day, and you need to ensure that the information in your estate plan is current.

Are You Ready?

It is essential to the well-being of your estate plan that you take each step of the process seriously. You should commit to spending time looking at what you need to do, deciding on the right solution to the problem, and implementing it. We will take you through each of those steps in detail.

You should also understand that planning an estate does take time. If you or someone you love is in need of a fast solution, contact an estate-planning attorney right away; this can speed up the process. In critical times, it is essential to implement fast decisions, but this does not mean that these decisions cannot be made with thorough consideration.

Now, it is time to begin your journey.

Three Spires of the Air Force Memorial, Arlington, Virginia

Chapter 2

What Are You Worth?

As part of the estate planning process, you will need to protect the possessions that you have. But if you do not know how much you have, or even what you have, this can be challenging.

In this chapter, we will look at the need and the process of calculating just what your estate is worth. You might find yourself surprised at your value. Most people do not realize what assets need to be included in their estate plan, and therefore, make the mistake of not including everything they have that has value. Mind you, we are not talking about determining who will get the shirt you are wearing or the pencil in your desk drawer. Rather, we are talking about items that have some sort of worth to them. For example, items such as real estate, vehicles, or assets in bank accounts or retirement plans should be included in your estate plan.

Most people think they know what they are worth, but most people are far off. This can be costly when it comes time to plan your estate because you might not take some items into account; or, even worse, you might fail to manage the tax deductions or costs that those items might have. That could be a real problem for you, ultimately.

In addition to this, you might have some debt. Big or small, this too factors into your worth, and you must determine just what it is and how it affects virtually every aspect of your estate plan.

The trick of estate planning is realizing that things change over time. If you are smart, you are planning your estate well before you reach old age. Even as you are planning, you will still find that factors will evolve and change; the value of your estate will inevitably vary over time. This too must be taken into consideration, today as well as in the future.

You need to have a foundation for success by planning your estate based on what you own, what you owe, and what changes will happen in the future. We will look at the various types of real property that you may have, and determine what it is worth.

What is Your Home Worth?

To get started, you need to consider your real property. Real property is the type of property that is tangible, including your home, for example. For most people, the home is the most valuable asset that they own in real property. Yet, do you know what your home is worth?

Unless you have purchased your home recently, you may not have a good understanding of the value that it has. That is because the value of your home has fluctuated, just as the real estate markets have moved quite a bit in the last several years.

In order to determine the value of your home, then, you need to do a bit of research. One of the best ways to understand the value of your home is to have a property appraiser come to your home and price it for you. This person's job is to know the value of the home. It is their job to compare your home to others in the area and what they have sold for over the last six months to a year. They will look at the size and details, and will walk through your home looking for benefits and disadvantages in order to get an accurate price for it. In addition, they will provide you with a good estimate of what you could get for your home if you sold it today. You can find a property appraiser in your area by looking in the phone book or conducting an Internet search.

The largest drawback to using an appraiser is that it will cost you somewhere between $250 up to $500 or more in some areas, but you will end up with an accurate price for your home to fairly split among your loved ones.

If you do not want to follow this route, find a quality, experienced real estate agent and talk to them. They can help you determine the value of a home as it would sell by looking solely at what your property features are in comparison to other homes in the area that have sold. They may charge you for this service, but it is likely to be less expensive than an appraiser. But you will also find that this is not as accurate of a description of your home's value either. Many people find real estate agents through word-of-mouth. Check with friends and family who have recently bought or sold property. You can also check your local phone book or search online.

You can ask for this information and then do the pricing yourself by comparing the homes in your area to your own for similarities. Yet, unless you know the value of features, the benefits of one neighborhood over the other, or the estimate of homes in general, this simply is not going to give you an accurate price for your home.

What Other Property is Out There?

Do you own any other type of property? Here are three types of real estate ownership situations in which you may already have property and therefore have to consider the value of this property for your real property valuation.

Timeshare: Do you own a timeshare? If you have a second home, or you own a part of that home, this is considered to be real property and something you need to know the value of. To determine the value of this type of property, you will need to follow the same basic principles as you did for your home's valuation.

Real estate partnerships: Do you have a partnership in which you and someone else own property? One such thing is that of a Limited Liability Company (LLC), or Limited Liability Partnerships (LLP). Here, you do not have direct ownership of the property, but you own it through these companies. This is a rather confusing aspect because the value of an LLC can go up and down quite a bit in just a year. In addition, you may be restricted on how and when you can sell it. To determine the value of one of these, you will need to know its worth based on where it is, what is there, and how these numbers change over time. You almost always need to have a professional give you the value of it, but you will likely need it to be reassessed as time goes by.

Real estate/landlord: Do you own land or property that you then rent to others? If so, this is an important piece of your real property. You could own a home that you rent to others, or you may own a part of an office building. These factors play a real role in the financial outlook of your estate and need to be carefully considered. You should have a commercial real estate appraiser look at the value of your property, or, if you know what you are doing, use the net operating income and capitalization rate of your property to determine the value of the land and property.

Land is one of the highest valued items for estate planning, but it is by far not the only real property that you have. In addition to this type of property, you need to know the value of other real property that you have.

Real Property beyond Real Estate

Both tangible and intangible properties need to have their value determined. This could be a process that takes you some time, but nevertheless, it must be done. You may want to work with your estate-planning attorney in determining the value of some of these items. While we will give you advice on how to do this here, it can fluctuate greatly.

Your personal property ranges significantly in value. Many of the items that you have, such as that pencil on your desk, have little to no value. So, why do you need to bother with tracking those differences? Why do you need to write down all the items that you have?

With estate planning, your goal is to provide for your loved ones, and even if you do not believe it, dividing your personal items among them — even the least in value — is a must. Therefore, while you are taking the time to list all your property for valuation needs, you should also be taking the time to list all your property in order to know who will get what. The following are some steps to help you to determine the best way to work through this:

- Work with your homeowner's insurance provider. Most homeowner's policies will require that you have a list of the items in your home in order to provide coverage for those items. Therefore, you can use the list you have already completed while planning your estate.

- List each item in your home in categories. To do this, you can use a spreadsheet on your computer or even just a piece of paper. A good way to do this is to go room-by-room. Start in your bedroom, for example.

- List all the items in your bedroom. Include those that have sentimental value, but not real monetary value (photos, the pin handed down from your grandmother); those that have monetary value (your furniture, artwork, and jewelry); and those that have no financial value or sentimental value (clothing, knick-knacks).
- Do not spend too much time on those items that have no value, but do spend time tracking the value of items that have some financial benefit to you. You should write down the estimated value of the item (more on how to do this in the next section).

Tips for valuing your "stuff"

Determining the value of your belongings is no doubt going to be a long process. But there are a few ways that you can make it less time-consuming.

First off, make an estimated guess for each object. If you do not have any idea of how much something is worth, you can use the Web to help you. Visit online retail stores or use online auctions to find out what a product just like yours is selling for. You want to get as close to the actual item as possible (factoring in age and certain features) to get an accurate estimate.

Another tip that makes the process of valuation faster is doing so with the help of your camera. You can take a picture of the item, figure the costs, and tape it onto the back of the photo. In any case, digital or not, pictures make the process faster. If you have a video recorder, this is even faster and can be just as effective as a piece of paper by allowing you to film everything in a room at once, rather than taking individual photos.

For sentimental items, try your best to put a value to these items, but realize the value will likely have depreciated greatly — or the item will have no value at all.

Do not forget the intangible

What we have talked about so far are the things that you can touch. But you have real property that extends beyond this level that needs to be taken note of. Each product you have needs to be evaluated to determine how it will affect your estate.

For most people, intangible property is the most valuable property they own. And, depending on what intangible property you own, it may be the easiest of all your property to valuate, which means that this part of the estate planning process is rather straightforward.

What is this type of property? Do you have stocks, bonds, mutual funds, annuities, savings accounts, or certificates of deposit (CD)? These are just a few of the examples that you need to take into consideration. Here is a checklist for you to determine what you have, where it is, and how much it is worth.

1. Determine all your assets that are intangible. List them and list where you have them. For example, you may have a savings account at one bank and a CD at another. Or you could have mutual funds that are spread out into several companies. Here, you need a list of what and where everything is. It makes sense to pull out all your paperwork and write down your account numbers, including the information you need to track the value of the item.

2. For some items, you just need to check your statement to know what the value of it is. To see how much you have in your savings

account, just check the statement. This can also go for your retirement accounts, your certificates of deposit, or other accounts like this that you may have.

3. If you have a broker who manages your money or investments, then you should meet with them to get a breakdown of the value that each investment has. Although you will be using a financial planner to manage your money, you still need to take into consideration what you have right now.

4. If you have stocks, you can learn their worth just by looking at the market at any given time. You should have a basic knowledge of the worth of each share and total shares that you have. You can also do this with mutual funds that you own. You can find them listed online or in your local newspaper. Remember, investments fluctuate frequently; their value could change day to day. The values will need to be updated within your estate plan regularly.

5. Interest payment schedules are also important for assets that have a long-term interest plan — for example, your savings account. Even more so, if you have a savings bond that will gradually increase in value, you will need to know what that increase is, both in what the value of the product is now and what it will be in the years to come.

What other intangible resources do you have, and if you were to sell them today, what value would they bring to you? Taking the steps right now to determine the answer will benefit you later.

Now you have determined what your property is, and should have a list of the different things that you own and their value listed next to them.

Even if you do not have an exact amount, you still know the basic idea of your worth.

But that is not your worth just yet. You counted all your assets, and now you need to get rid of the debt that you owe on this positive balance.

Your Debts: Subtracting Debt from Property

You need to take away the amount of money that you owe from the assets that you own. By doing this, you will be able to come to a true understanding of what your estate is worth. Just as we did with your property values, you now need to invest the time in determining what you owe. Here is a breakdown of all that you need to take into consideration.

Loans

The largest loan that most people have is their home. If you have a mortgage, a tax lien, or any other type of loan on your home, you will need to find out what the balance is. To determine the amount of money that you owe on your home, request a statement from your mortgage holder or your bank. This will provide you with several numbers, including the interest that you are being charged on the loan, which you will need later. You should know your monthly payment, the amount of years or payments you have left, and the total that you owe on the home mortgage (any and all that you have).

Do you have student loans? Do you have loans on your car? These all need to be considered in the same manner. Learn what the balance is, what your interest rate is, what you pay monthly, and the number of payments left until the debt is paid in full. If you have loans on any property, such as recreational vehicles, 401(k) loans, or debts that you owe to others, include them here in the same manner.

Credit cards

The other costly debt that some people have is that of credit cards. Take time to go through all your credit card accounts and list what you owe on each one. Here, you should also write down the costs of the cards in interest, monthly payment amounts, as well as the total amount owed. This will help you to determine the amount that you owe.

With credit cards, the amount that you owe can go up and down quite a bit. It will ultimately be a factor in why you use the credit that you have. Determine the amount that you owe, realizing that this will change month by month, depending on your credit usage.

Make sure to include all the charge accounts that you have, which will include bank cards, credit lines through retailers, your home equity lines of credit, and any other accounts that you have that allow you to charge your purchase. Some credit accounts do not have an actual credit card, but rather, you will write checks for the amount you wish to draw out. Consider these in the same regard.

Your future debts

While you cannot know for sure what you will spend in the future, you can clearly see what the costs are in relation to some big expenses. For example, if you plan to pay for your child's education through college, you know that this will be a substantial debt. Your future debts can include any large expenses that you know are coming.

On that same token, you should take into consideration the amount of money you will be saving down the road, too. For example, if you have only a handful of payments left until your home is paid in full, you should consider this debt just as you would any other. But you should realize that you will have to readjust this amount within that time period as a positive balance account.

Do the math

Now that you have it all figured out on paper, you can easily do the math and come up with the best plan for you.

Take the amount of real property value that you have and subtract it from the cost of your debt. By totaling all these beforehand, you know clearly what your property value and your debts are, and you can subtract the debts and see what you are worth.

Are you scared of that number? Are you worried that it is not enough? For some, it may even be a negative balance. Instead of worrying about this right now, consider the long-term value of these items, as it is likely to increase over time. For that, you need to consider the long-term outlook on your debt, as we will do in the next section.

What Does the Future Hold in Worth?

You may think that you have a good net worth, or perhaps not. But what you must realize is that this number changes. If you spend $1,000, that affects your net worth. If you pay off a vehicle, then your asset value rises and your debts fall. As you can see, managing your estate plan in terms of net worth is critical, and it is something you have to do on a regular basis. It will be necessary for you to track these changes annually and readjust your estate plan to fit your current situation.

Not only does the financial aspect of your estate plan change quite a bit, but so does your life. Just think back ten years ago. What were you doing? Have you gotten married in that time? Perhaps you have had two children in the last ten years. You may have changed jobs, improved your income, or purchased stocks. Each of these events plays a role in the outlook of your estate plan.

Should you have a large life change happen to you, you need to come back to your estate plan, especially your net worth, and make changes to it to reflect that information.

This can be especially important in situations such as getting married, getting divorced, and having children. The drastic changes that happen here are critical to your estate outlook. Changes affect not only your net worth, but also the way that your estate is divided among your family.

Many people think they are giving their children what they deserve by splitting inheritance equally among them. Then, when they pass away, one sibling ends up with more than the other. The reason is that the value of stocks, investments, and even the value of a home may have changed. One child may get more than the other. Then, siblings who were supposed to be provided equally for end up with different amounts of assets and value.

As you can see, it is vital to go back to your assets and determine what they are worth currently. This way, you get to leave your property and assets to those whom you want to have them, based on their value right now.

Now that you know your net worth, we can move into the dividing up of those assets to help protect your loved ones when you die. This process is called a will.

Factoring in Settlement Costs

One of the key points of estate planning is preparing yourself for the costs associated with the settlement of your estate. Settlement costs consist of taxes and fees that will be required to carry out your estate. Your heirs or those who are in your estate plan will have to pay these costs. These costs should be kept in mind along with your actual estate value.

Here are a few settlement costs that should be considered, and later planned for, in your estate:

- The cost of your last illness, medical stay, or care for the last days or months of your life.
- The cost of your funeral, embalming and/or cremation, and burial.
- The cost of any debts incurred that are not paid for at the time of your death.
- Probate administration expenses. These can include anything from court costs to the preparation of final documents for court proceedings and attorney fees.
- Death taxes, or estate taxes, which you will learn more about in Chapter 8, are tax levied on the value of your property.

The goal of estate planning is to plan for and minimize any and all of these costs as much as possible. Settlement costs can be enormous, especially when the value of your estate exceeds the estate tax threshold. Even for someone who has little in the way of value, settling an estate can be a pricey situation, costing most families thousands of dollars.

Yet you can plan for most of these expenses, and the rest of this book delves into how to do so.

Capitol Building, Richmond, Virginia

Chapter 3

Your Will: The Definition of Your Estate Plan

You have seen it in movies and on television shows: The family of a wealthy relative is meeting, anticipating what they are being given in the will. They are eagerly sitting there, pretending to have cared about dear old Uncle John and telling stories about how much he touched their lives, even though they have not spoken to him in at least four years. The meeting concerns his will and how much will be given to each of them.

In reality, it is more likely you cannot wait for the moment when your loved ones will receive all you have worked hard for. No matter what you are dreaming about, the will is an essential piece of legal work that should not be skipped.

It is so important that we have included it here, toward the beginning of the estate plan. No matter if you want your pet dog to get it all, or if you want to give everything to charity, your last will defines what you want to give, where you want it to go, and how you want your last wishes carried out.

The key to a will is to keep it up-to-date about you and your life. A will that is clearly defined and current is the best piece of legal work that you have that can be used to honor your wishes. With the help of a will, you will be able to precisely define your loved ones' futures.

If you forget to go back to your will and include your newest grandchild, or you forget to make changes to your child's college education requirements, they may end up losing out. If something changes down the road, include it in your will. You should come back to your estate plan (including your will) each year to consult it and consider any necessary changes that need to be made.

Even worse are the mistakes that can occur when it comes to making a will. If you do not include a skilled estate planning attorney in the development of your will, you will find yourself in even more hot water. The terminology and legal clauses that go into will planning can be quite difficult to understand and will likely confuse anyone without a law degree.

The goal of a will is to define who will get what, but a simple error in the wording can put you in the position of not being able to avoid estate taxes, or it may include wording that can be contested, which means your heirs can fight the terms you set forth. The end result is that a court of law defines your last wishes rather than you. It cannot be said enough that a quality estate planning attorney should be used to define your will.

One important definition that you need to take into consideration is that of a beneficiary. As you will see throughout this chapter, a beneficiary is the person who will profit from your will. For example, if you name your children as beneficiaries, they will get something from your will, as you set its terms. Heirs, businesses, and even charities can be beneficiaries in your will.

A will can be the sole piece of work you do to protect your heirs. While an entire estate plan is the best route to take to fully care for your estate, you can simply have a will. There are several people whom this can benefit. For example, if you are healthy and young, you may want to get certain things down in writing for "just in case" situations. For many, this means caring for their children in the event of a crisis.

Or, if you do need an estate plan and have not had the time to develop one just yet, a will allows you to buy some time until you get your estate plan done. At least write your will, because it will define exactly what you want to happen when you die — even though only having a will means that your estate is likely to end up in probate, leaving a court to decide how your assets will be divided.

Your Will is a Backup

In the estate planning process, a will can be a backup piece of paper to your trust. There are a number of times when your will can help you to better define what you will be leaving and to whom you will leave it. Here are some times when having a will happens to be the better decision than having just a trust for your estate.

- Some property is better left in a will. For example, the car you own or the frequent flier miles that you have are better off in a will than in a trust because it is too hard for these items to be managed through a trust. Most car insurance companies will not provide insurance to a car that is in a trust.

- If you happen to win the lottery, and then you pass away, this extra and unexpected property is something you will want to give to those that you love, but who gets it? If you have not had the opportunity to get a change made to your estate plan, a will can be helpful. In this example, if you died just a few weeks after winning the lottery (would that not be your luck?), then the winnings of the lottery would be forwarded to the person named in your will as the residuary beneficiary. A residuary beneficiary receives everything that is not specifically named in your will for someone else.

- If you are a parent of a minor child or children at the time of your death, your will can be a vehicle for naming your preference for their guardianship. Virginia provides this option for a sole parent. This provision in your will advises the court of your preference; it is advisable to state your reasons so that the court will have the benefit of understanding your choice of guardian. This is especially important if your choice supersedes someone who would normally be the guardian next in line by law, as the child's next of kin. In Virginia, naming a guardian for your children if you are their sole parent will likely carry great weight. If they have a surviving parent, though, that parent will have primary parental right of guardianship absent a compelling reason to the contrary. Simply attempting to override the other parent in your will is not likely to work, unless all parties consent to the Court's satisfaction. This is a tricky issue that you must discuss with your legal counsel if you have it in mind.

- Perhaps you want to disinherit someone in your estate because you do not want them to receive anything — the only way for you to do this is through a will. You can legally do this with a spouse or with a child. There are laws that govern this, though, that you need to know about.

- You will use your will to name your executor, too. We will discuss this later in this chapter.

- If you know that you will own something in the future, and want to make sure that it is divided the way that you want, then a will is a must. A will can include a clause that includes property that you believe is coming to you at some time in the future.

As you can see, there are some things that a will can do for you that your general estate plan cannot. You will want to invest the time necessary in getting this worked out with an attorney to ensure that your wishes come true.

Getting Your Will Started

As we have talked about, you need to have an estate planning professional, preferably an attorney, to handle the development of your will. This person should work closely with you to ensure that all your needs are met during the planning of the will. Once you have them selected, you can start forming your will.

First and foremost, you should find out your legal estate tax. You will learn more about this later, but for now, just realize that it should be one of the first subjects that you talk about with your attorney. You need to know just how much money your estate will need to pay out in taxes when you die so that this amount is set aside for just that purpose and does not affect the items that you want to give to those you are leaving behind.

You know your net worth, and you know what belongs to you and its value. Whom you want to leave your money to is a personal decision, and one that you should not make on your own, but with your spouse and loved ones. Nevertheless, it is your money to do with what you see fit.

Take a moment to write down who you want to leave something to. Do you want to include all your children? Do you want your brothers, sisters, and your friend down the street to receive payments? You have to decide not only who gets your funds, but also who you do not want to get a share. You may not want one of your children to receive any of your possessions.

For many, there is also a desire to provide your estate, or at least part of it, to charity. Perhaps you want the funds from your estate to go toward funding a new park in your neighborhood. If you do want such things to happen, then you need to decide this now.

At this point, you may not know what or how much you want to leave each of those you love. Before you begin to figure that out, you should take some time to determine just what your options are, which means learning a bit more about wills. You will learn that here, of course, but for now, plan a meeting with your attorney to discuss whom you want to include in your will and what the goals of your will are. The legalities of the setup will depend on the goals that you have.

What makes a will legal?

An important consideration is the legality of a will. No matter if you have every good intention, there are laws in place that can limit and restrict what you are doing. There are some rules that make a will legal; in other words, if they are not fulfilled, then your will simply will not go through.

Here are some things that are required in order for your will to be considered a legal document:

- In Virginia, a person age 18 or older is of legal age to make a will, as is a person emancipated at a younger age. Virginia law provides a procedure for persons age 16 to 18 to be declared emancipated.
- You must be of sound mind. Although this is continually contested in television soap operas, it is not likely that this will be

something contested in real life — without real proof. Your attorney may go through a series of tests, or they may have a doctor sign off on this if you are concerned that someone would contest your will on these grounds.

- In Virginia, you may write your will out by hand, type it, or print it out from your computer. Virginia recognizes a "holographic" will — that is, a document made entirely in your own handwriting and signed. Although witnesses are not required on a holographic will, Virginia will require that two witnesses verify that the handwriting is yours.

- You must have a date on the will of when it was created and signed.

- You must name a person to be the executor — referred to in Virginia as a "personal representative" — of your will. It is recommended that you also name a backup executor, as a contingency in case your first-named person cannot serve (or prefers not to serve) for some reason.

- You must list at least one substantive provision. For example, you must leave your property to a named person in your will.

One of your estate planning attorney's roles is to ensure that you have covered all the necessary requirements for a valid will.

Choosing your executor

The executor of your will is the person who will make sure that your wishes are carried out. There are many people who can be chosen for this job, but the best person to choose is the one whom you trust the most. If you name a person as executor of your will, you trust them to make the right decisions about your hard-earned money. You are giving them the ability to have those wishes carried out, and also to consider any necessary work that goes along with the process.

When it comes to naming your executor, consider several factors. First, you can have several people do the job. This does make things much more complicated, though, because they will all need to handle the responsibility and make decisions together. This may be a good idea, though, if you will be causing a family fight or conflict if you name just one person as your executor.

Once you have selected the right person for the job, you need to make sure it is all right with them, because the tasks of being an executor can be somewhat time-consuming and quite a bit of responsibility. Do not be offended if the person you choose does not feel he or she is the right person for the job.

All wills legally require one executor to be appointed in them. One option that you have is to hire someone to execute your will that is not a "someone." Consider hiring a company or a bank to manage your estate after you die. While this technically sounds like a good thing, it does leave the personal touch off, which means decisions are based solely on getting the job done. That also means that they will likely charge fees for everything that they do for you.

The executor of your will is responsible for getting your probate taken care of, as well as supervising the property and funds transfers to those you have deemed deserve it. He or she also has to take into consideration the estate tax that you may be owed and file these payments. Your estate attorney should be able to help them through the process, but officially, the executor makes these decisions.

What type of will is the right will?

You will be working with your estate planning attorney to create your will, but you should still realize the different types of wills and what they mean to you. You do have the option of using them, should they fit your need.

Simple wills

A simple will is the most common type of will today. These wills are not joint wills, as they serve only for one person. In addition, they are a single piece of documentation that describes your wishes. When this type of will is used, it will state that the document is your will. It will list your beneficiaries, including any charities, and their addresses and birth dates. In addition, it will name the executor of your will and possibly a secondary executor in case the first cannot provide for you. It will also include your directions for who will care for your children and your property, as well as distribute your assets as you direct.

Handwritten wills

You may have heard of the term "holographic will." This is a completely handwritten will signed only by the testator, without witnesses. A few states recognize this type of will; Virginia is one of them. Although you can technically have this type of handwritten will in Virginia, it is one of the most troublesome types of wills that you can have. If you do take this route, you will need to have the will written out completely.

The problem with holographic wills is that the probate judge may worry that it is not the wishes of the person that wrote it, but rather was forged. The handwritten will can also lead to a number of concerns about the proof that is required for the will to be considered legal. How will your heirs prove that you wrote it, or the authenticity of the date? Handwriting expertise may be called into service in a will contest. Therefore, it would be best for you to type or write a will and have the required witnesses watch you sign it and sign their names under yours, if at all possible.

Exigent circumstances sometimes do make the holographic will an important option where it is allowed. The most well-known cases historically have been those on battlefields, at accident scenes, and involving people in isolation for some reason. There are circumstances where they have proved effective. Out of concern for such exceptions, the holographic will law has remained in place in Virginia.

Joint wills

A joint will is a type of will that two people, usually a husband and wife, write together as one document. This is not a common practice because the will becomes not only a last will and testament, but a contract between the two people who have made it. Normally, if you make your will, you have the right to change it or add to it, or completely revoke it in favor of a new one. If you make a joint will with another, you may be giving up your right to revoke the will. You might argue that property you acquired after making that joint will is not covered by it, but that argument will be subject to a court's decision ultimately. For these reasons, joint wills are not the recommended approach. There are much better methods for spouses and life partners to arrange their estate planning. Virginia statutes do not reference joint wills.

Mutual wills

Another type of will that you may be able to use is a mutual will. In this type of will, two people can have their wills or estate plans linked together — for example, if you and someone else have been working on a project for a long time and you want your assets or a portion of them to go to the project you have been working on. So, you can set up your will to include specialized amounts to be donated depending on who dies first. You can split money among several organizations this way so that no matter who dies first, the most important charity or organization gets those funds first. The legalities of this type of will are important to understand, though, so ensure that you work with an attorney who knows the ins and outs of mutual wills.

Ethical wills

If you have something to say to your loved ones, then an ethical will may be a wise choice. Usually, an ethical will is one that is done separately from your legal will. It allows you the ability to talk about your thoughts, feelings, concerns, and values. You can use it to tell stories about events that were important, life-altering situations, or you can use it to help you share your thoughts on why you gave one person money and the next nothing.

Sometimes, people want to use ethical wills to make stipulations on their heir's ability to cash in on the estate. For example, you may put in your will that unless your grandson finishes college, he does not get anything from your estate. While this can be something that you technically can do, it becomes difficult to enforce. Even more so, someone has to take the time to understand what your goals are and to help make sure that the end result is achieved. You will also need to have a trust in place to manage these funds for the time being.

Other types of wills

Although the wills we have already mentioned are rarely used — except for the simple will — the following wills are additional options that you have that can be even more limiting. Most states, including Virginia, have strict laws on these types of wills that you must know about before you attempt to use them.

- **Nuncupative**: This will, also known as an oral will, is one that is spoken. The only time that this will can be used, in most cases, is when someone is on his or her deathbed. If you are going to die within minutes, this type of will can be used in highly unusual circumstances. Virginia law does not recognize nuncupative wills.

- **International will**: Some states provide for certification of international wills, using procedures prescribed by the Uniform International Wills Act. Virginia statutes describe the form to recognize an international will.

- **Electronic wills**: Another type of will that has been appearing recently is the electronic will. Only Nevada allows this type of will, though. If a Nevada resident has created a will in electronic format, such as on the computer, this could be an option, but it is not that easy. In addition to the actual electronic recording, there must be a way of identifying who wrote the will, which could include fingerprints, retinal scans, or even voice recognition. Sometimes it is required to have a specialized program to write the will that includes an electronic signature.

- **Video wills**: You see these all the time on television, but no state allows a will to be video-recorded as the sole way of communicating your wishes. You can recite your wishes over video and communicate your needs through video, but only if you also have a legal document in place. This is a good addition to your legal will, though, especially when you believe that the will might be contested.

Now that we have gone through a wide range of wills, you have to realize that the only fail-safe type of will is a simple will. You should only use these other wills in extreme conditions in which they work for your special circumstances. Talk with your attorney to learn whether one of them may be a fitting choice for you.

Developing a Will

Now that you have a good understanding of what type of will you need, it is time to consider the legal inclusions in that will. What you must take into consideration is the need to have a will that is legally binding. Without the inclusion of the right things and the right wording in your will, it can be contested by your heirs or even by the judge in probate. That is what you want to avoid if you can.

Throughout the document, there are going to be different sections and terms used to help get your wishes represented clearly. These wishes are organized into clauses throughout the will. With the right clauses, your wishes can be easily understood and clearly defined.

Clauses make up the important part of your will, and therefore, there are many of them. You need to know what these clauses are and what they mean. Lucky for us, it is easy to break them down and explain them.

Opening clauses

The first type of clause is an opening clause. It provides the opening to your will, which includes your identification and any information that is necessary to move into the actual body of the will. The opening clause also makes a statement about your free will in making the will and describes you as being of sound mind. In some circumstances, such as a person who is on serious pain medication, being of sound mind may require the lawyer to ask a series of questions, or a doctor to sign off on mental state.

In many states, simply making a new will automatically revokes a prior one. It is not so clear in Virginia. Virginia Code section 64.1-58.1 states:

> "If a testator executes a will or other writing in the manner in which a will is required to be executed, and such will or other writing expressly revokes a previous will, such previous will, including any codicil thereto, is thereby void and of no effect.
>
> If a testator duly executes a will or codicil which does not expressly revoke a former will or codicil, but which expressly revokes a part thereof, or contains provisions inconsistent therewith, such former will or codicil is revoked and superseded to the extent of such express revocation or inconsistency if the later will or codicil becomes effectual upon the death of the testator."

This means that parts of a prior will that are not inconsistent with the new will in some way will be read together with the new will and not be considered "revoked." The result could be something you did not intend or anticipate because you assumed the prior will was void.

Therefore the opening clause of your Virginia will must be very clear about your intent as to how the will affects any prior will you may have made, including a will you may have executed in a different state. If you are preparing a new will in its entirety, the best approach is to expressly state that all previous wills are expressly revoked, void, and of no effect — words that echo those of the Virginia statute.

In the opening clause, you will also identify those who are listed or included in some way in your will later on. Here, you might simply introduce them as "my sister Betty," for example.

In addition, there is usually a tax clause entered into this part of your will. This clause will help define what your tax strategy is, and how you want those taxes to be paid on your estate. As we will discuss in Chapter 8, doing this is important to protecting your heirs, as well as protecting your estate. Adding the tax information here will help to deliver the information your heirs need from the start.

Giving clauses

Now it is time to do the work of your will. The giving clause is the area of your will that comes after your opening clause and describes the meat of the will. Here, you get to name who is going to get your furniture, your home, and your other property. This part of the will is where you get to name your wishes, and for that reason, you should consider it as being one of the most important parts of your will and even your estate plan.

The giving clause should be well-worded. It should include all necessary information clearly presented without any assumptions. The good news is that you get to choose just how specific you want to be in the will. For some people, just being general about the gifts that they are giving is good enough. For others, it is important to be extremely detailed in each aspect of the will's gifts. Or, you can use a combination of these things; for example, you may want to specifically include information about your high-priced book collection, but you may not care as much about your furniture and clothing.

One route that you can take with your giving clause is to simply say that you would like all your property and your net worth to be divided among those whom you name as beneficiaries equally. You may want to do this if you do not have specific needs and desires to divide your property among your loved ones. In this case, your net worth, whatever it is, will be divided equally among your heirs.

If you do not want an equal portion of your will to go to each of your heirs, then you need to be as precise and detailed as you can be about who is going to get what. Doing this will help your wishes to be completely understood — instead of allowing people to fight over each item that you own. It can also be important to do this if you have a large, extended family and want certain people to get better gifts than others, or you want each person to get a specific item.

Now, there are three different types of giving clauses that you need to take into consideration for the types of giving that you plan to do. These clauses are in place to directly provide for your wishes:

- **Personal property clause**: The first of these is a personal property clause. Your personal property (as we have described in earlier sections) is both your tangible and your intangible property. In this part of the will, you need to include specific directions about what will happen to your personal items. This should include your valuable and sentimental property. In most cases, it will be important to you to list who gets the family heirlooms or other important items that you are leaving behind.

- **Real property clause**: Again, your real property is, monetarily, the most valuable part of your estate. In this case, you will want to divide up the property among those that you want to own it. This clause identifies what your real property is and tells of your wishes about who will get that property or how it will be divided. In most cases, people are specific about this type of property simply because of the value that it has.

- **Residuary clause**: The third part of your giving clause is that of the residuary clause. This type of clause is important, especially if you

> do not take the time to come back and make changes to your will as you should. It will determine exactly who gets whatever else you have not mentioned in your will. For example, if you write up your will today and include your son Max as the residuary beneficiary, then he would get anything that is not listed specifically in other areas of your will. If you purchase a boat in the next year and die without including something specific in your will about the boat, Max would inherit the boat because of this power. This clause is essential simply because if the will is not updated, or you forget to mention something, it is a catch-all for the rest of your belongings.

As a side note, there are additional clauses in your giving clause that help to define exactly who will manage your estate and what powers they will have. These clauses are called the appointment clause and the fiduciary powers clause. There are additional clauses as well, which have little to do with the actual estate you are planning to take care of. Instead, they may be legal terminology that just has to be there but does not affect the way that you hand out your estate.

Ending clause

Now that you have your wishes spelled out in the giving clauses, you can end your will. You have given away your property, and you have specifically described everything that you want to happen when you die. Now, it is time to sign on the dotted line. The ending clause provides for the signature — in its own separate clause, called the signature clause, of course. In addition, your witnesses will need to sign your will at this point. The date will also need to be placed in this clause.

When you sign your will, you state that you are doing so by your own free will and of sound mind. When your witnesses sign your will, they are attesting to the fact that you are not being forced to sign it in any way and that they are witnesses to the action. Your witnesses cannot be listed as beneficiaries in your will. These people need to be people who do not benefit from your will in any way.

Now, there is the matter of probate to consider here. You can avoid the need to provide witnesses during probate if you select and have your witnesses sign correctly. This is called having the will "self proved." To do this, you will need to have the witnesses' signatures done in a specific way. First, they will need to have their signatures acknowledged as well as being witnesses. You also need them to provide affidavits stating that they saw this happen and signed your will. When this is done, probate will not require that your witnesses come forward stating that they saw you sign your will.

And that is it; that is what goes into the will. Of course, the process of determining who will get what can be more challenging and ultimately will take you the most time. Yet it is fundamentally necessary to go through each of your needs carefully so that you do not forget something that can cost you — or, rather, cost your loved ones — dearly.

What Cannot be Included in a Will?

This book describes the process of developing an estate plan, which is much more than just managing your will. In an estate plan, you will work to develop a plan for everything that you own and wish to happen when you die. But a will is an excellent part of that estate plan because it can define much of what you are looking to have spelled out. Although a will can do quite a bit for your estate plan, it cannot do everything.

There are a number of items that cannot be included in your will. Your estate plan will cover most of these things, but you still need to know what you cannot put in your will.

If you list any of your property in another part of your estate planning or place other ownership on the property, then it cannot be included in your will. If it is included there, the ownership remains dependent on the other form instead of on the directions you provide in your will. Your attorney will tell you specifically what can and cannot be included for your special circumstances, but here is a general list of property that, if placed in other parts of your estate plan, cannot be placed in your will.

- **A living trust**: A living trust is something we will talk about later in Chapter 7, but for this purpose, anything that you put into a living trust will be executed to those individuals as the trust deems, not your will.

- **Life insurance**: If you have a life insurance plan set up that is payable to a beneficiary, the funds must go to that beneficiary, not to those listed in your will.

- **Joint tenancy property**: If you die and leave a spouse behind, the share that is yours goes to them. If you are the last to die, then you can put this property into your will.

- **Pay-on-death accounts**: If you set up an account that pays out when you die, then the person named to receive those funds in the account paperwork will get them, not the person you name in your will.

- **Other accounts**: If you have retirement accounts, 401(k)s, or other accounts like this that have funds in them at the time of your death, those funds go to the person or people named as your beneficiary, not to those whom you name in the will.

If you do not want the person listed as your beneficiary on these types of accounts to get your funds, then you need to consider making changes to the accounts. Talk to your life insurance provider and get this changed. Contact the holders of your other accounts and fix this problem now, because your will cannot do it for you.

Additional Will Contents and Concerns

The process of making a will is a bit more complicated than what it seems here. In the next chapter, we will talk about the legal aspects of the will, including some important aspects. But there are a few parts of the will that we have not talked about that should be mentioned here. Take into consideration these aspects of the will's make-up as well. You may find it necessary to add these things into your will.

Explanations: Feel the need?

If you feel that it is important to tell those whom you love why you did what you did in your will, then do just that. Leaving explanatory letters that will accompany your will is often a good idea, especially for those who face worries about what their heirs will think.

To get this letter started, you will first start with an explanation of what the letter is. It will help to clarify what you want done with the letter, as well as help those who are handling your death understand what it is. There is no real legality to these types of letters, but they can be somewhat confusing if the person does not know full well what they are getting into. The fact is that having this letter done can help you to feel better about the decisions that you make in your will.

You do not have to write this type of letter, but if you have feelings, thoughts, or expressions that you would like to make, this letter is a good place to do so. You may want to explain to your family and friends why you left the money, property, or other items in your will to those whom you did. This can be a good way to talk about why it was important to you to give that old piece of art to your daughter, and why you wanted to give your son money.

Although, legally, you do not have to do this, it can be helpful to talk about what you are giving your loved ones before you die. You can sit down and thoroughly talk about why someone is getting more than another person, and why you feel it is important. Even if you do this — or if you do not — you may want to define why you did not give out your property evenly to all your heirs. No matter if you make the decision to leave your property unevenly distributed because you have already given out a large amount of your money to one person and not to another, or because you feel someone has a greater need, you may want to clarify this now in a letter.

Another reason to leave this type of letter is to talk about your feelings. Perhaps you want to explain why you are leaving all your money to your favorite charity. Perhaps you want to tell someone what he or she meant to you during your lifetime. You may want to communicate a number of sentiments and gratitude to those that you are leaving behind. There does not have to be any types of corollary to this and what you leave in your will, though.

One thing that people are sometimes tempted to do is to leave bad sentiments and feelings to those whom they may not have liked all that much. It may feel beneficial to do this when you feel the urge, but you may want to consider not doing so. Legally speaking, there is no reason why you cannot; but you may want to save those sentiments for a less public forum.

Finally, this letter is also a tool to help you express your needs and desires for those you leave behind, from children to pets. You can easily remark on these subjects here so that those who are caring for these important parts of your life do so with the best of wishes and trust. Again, nothing here is legally binding, but it can be the perfect place to state your wishes in this regard.

Pets and wills

If you love your pets and want to make sure that they are taken care of when you die, then you can include information regarding them in your will. There are a number of actions that you can take, but there are also considerations that must be made about what you cannot do. Beyond anything else, you cannot leave money or property to your pet directly. What you can do, though, is to provide for your pet through other methods.

Your pet is considered property, not a beneficiary. That means that you will need to set up care for your pet. If you attempt to leave property or a trust for your pet, it will likely be given to your residuary beneficiary, and not to the pet.

There are two ways you can provide for a pet following your death. One way is to name a person in your will as a beneficiary who gets ownership and possession of the pet, along with a sum of money for the pet's care. For obvious reasons, this needs to be someone you trust to care for the pet, someone with whom you have discussed this plan when you made your will.

Another approach permitted in Virginia is to set up a pet trust. Trusts, in general, are discussed later on in Chapter 7. For pets, Virginia Code section 55-544.08, the "pet trust" statute, provides the following:

> "A. A trust may be created to provide for the care of an animal alive during the settlor's lifetime. The trust terminates upon the death

of the animal or, if the trust was created to provide for the care of more than one animal alive during the settlor's lifetime, upon the death of the last surviving animal. Funds from the trust may be applied to any outstanding expenses of the trust and for burial or other postdeath expenditures for animal beneficiaries as provided for in the instrument creating the trust.

B. The instrument creating the trust shall be liberally construed to bring the transfer within the scope of trusts governed by this section, to presume against the merely precatory or honorary nature of the disposition, and to carry out the general intent of the transferor. Extrinsic evidence is admissible in determining the transferor's intent.

C. A trust authorized by this section may be enforced by a person appointed in the terms of the trust or, if no person is so appointed, by a person appointed by the court. A person having an interest in the welfare of the animal may request the court to appoint a person to enforce the trust or to remove a person appointed. The appointed person shall have the rights of a trust beneficiary for the purpose of enforcing the trust, including receiving accountings, notices, and other information from the trustee and providing consents. Reasonable compensation for a person appointed by the court may be paid from the assets of the trust.

D. Except as ordered by a court or required by the trust instrument, no filing, report, registration, periodic accounting, separate maintenance of funds, appointment, or surety bond shall be required by reason of the existence of the fiduciary relationship of the trustee.

E. Property of a trust authorized by this section may be applied only to its intended use, except to the extent the court determines that

> the value of the trust property exceeds the amount required for the intended use. Except as otherwise provided in the terms of the trust, property not required for the intended use shall be distributed to the settlor, if then living. If the settlor is deceased, such property shall be distributed pursuant to the residuary clause of the settlor's will if the trust for the animal was created in a preresiduary clause in the will or pursuant to the residuary provisions of the inter vivos trust if the trust for the animal was created in a preresiduary clause in the trust instrument; otherwise, such property shall be distributed to the settlor's successors in interest."

The statute makes clear that your intent to set up a trust for your animals' benefit will be liberally interpreted in favor of providing for the animal's care, in an amount the court deems reasonable for the animals care, so long as it lives. Beyond that, the funds left over will pass to those whom you have designated as residuary beneficiaries either in the trust or your will.

The key is to work with an experienced trust attorney to ensure you have covered your bases to set up this mechanism to care for your pet(s).

Who will fight my will? Will they win?

With the drama of television and movies, many are afraid that the will they put so much thought and heart into, containing their wishes and their needs, may somehow be contested and will end up meaning nothing. Although this worry is there for a good reason — because you can have your will contested — it is rare that anyone will win this type of legal proceeding.

The only factors that can make your will null and void are the things we have talked about. If you are over the age of 18, have made the will without any coercion or under duress, and are mentally fit, then there is little chance that your will can be successfully contested. It is quite difficult to prove such allegations, too. The burden of proof is on the person who is claiming it, not on the court. A court will not say that a person is incapable of making his or her own decision unless there is clear evidence of unsound mind. In addition, unless there is proof of something being quite wrong, it is highly unlikely that the will can be changed.

Even still, you may be concerned. The good news is that your lawyer can help make your will stronger so that it will not be contested. He or she may recommend certain legal filings that will provide additional protection to you. If you are unable to sign your name or have other conditions in which you cannot communicate, a good attorney will be more than willing to help you, and in some cases, can write your name for you. An attorney can also testify for you on grounds that he or she knew your competence at the time of the will signing. Meet with and consider talking to someone about this as soon as possible, especially if there is a large amount of property that is in question.

Keep your will safe

Now that your will is written, you need to keep it safe. There is much debate about where you should you put it and what should you do to it. Some attorneys feel strongly about this decision, and it makes good sense to follow what they say.

First, the original will is the most important piece of paper. This has the actual signatures on it that make it authentic. This piece of paper should be kept secured and carefully protected.

- Many people mistakenly believe a bank safety deposit box is the best place to tuck away a will for safekeeping. While it is a reasonably safe place, it may not be a readily accessible place after your death for probate. In Virginia, the safety deposit box can be accessed to determine if it contains a will, but the process is formal and cumbersome. Virginia Code section 6.1-332.1 provides several provisions related to the process, depending on whether a person is deceased or incapacitated due to illness (as certified by a physician). In the event of death, the statute summarizes how the process works as follows:

"Upon the death of a sole lessee of a safe-deposit box, the company or bank may permit limited access to the box by the spouse or next of kin of the deceased lessee or by a court clerk or other interested person for the limited purpose of looking for a will or other testamentary instruments. Access shall be under the supervision of a designated officer or employee, and nothing shall be removed from the box except the will or testamentary instrument for transmission to the appropriate clerk."

A co-lessee can access the safety deposit box because that person has access of right. If the co-lessee is not available, the above process can still be applied to access the box to search for a will.

- Virginia law prescribes a method for depositing your will during your lifetime with the clerk of court in the county in which you reside. Virginia Code section 64.1-56 states: "Any person or his attorney for him may, during his lifetime, lodge for safekeeping with the clerk of a court having probate jurisdiction in the county or city of his residence any will executed by such person; and the clerk shall thereupon receive such will and give the person lodging it a receipt therefor. The clerk shall then place the will in an envelope and seal it securely, numbering the envelope and endorsing thereon the name of the testator and the date on which it is so lodged, and shall index the same alphabetically in a permanent index kept for the purpose, showing therein the number and date such will is so deposited. The fee for such lodging, indexing, and preserving shall be two dollars, which shall be paid to the clerk when the will is received."

- If you want to keep your will with your attorney, you can do that also. He or she should be able to provide you with a safe at his office. You can also leave instructions on what to do when you die so as to not involve anyone else in the decision.

You should appoint someone your personal representative and executor. He or she should receive a copy of your will. Only your attorney should make these copies for you, though. Some people also like to give a copy of their will to several people, namely those listed in your will. This is fine, too, because it helps them to make plans for your death in advance, so there are no surprises for them later.

Finally, you should have an unsigned copy of your will with you at home. You will need to return to your will several times to ensure that it is still up-to-date and accurate in the information that it provides. This means that you will want to have a copy that you can reference. This copy can be used to make notes on, to discuss with your attorney later.

You do not have to tell anyone that you have signed your will; you do not have to tell anyone where your will is, except for your executor. But it is always best to leave surprises out of your will.

Lost, spoliated, or destroyed will

What if, despite all your efforts, your will cannot be found at the time of your death; it is inadvertently destroyed; or someone has interfered with it? If it can be proved that a copy of the will is true and accurate under such circumstances, especially where there is evidence someone interfered with a valid will, the court will likely accept the copy for probate. In Virginia, the fact of a will registered with the court would be useful evidence that a will existed. Although the registry does not provide for a copy on record, the registration of the will puts its existence, date, time, and location on record. The registration will be helpful to proving a copy is a valid substitute for a lost, spoliated, or destroyed will.

This is a situation in which having placed a copy of your executed will with your attorney or the person you named as your executor would have been a smart precaution. The copy will show that you signed a document that has the words showing it to be a will, and that there were witnesses. The witnesses can be called upon to verify there was an original.

Keep them out

If there are people whom you plan to keep out of your will, then you should list them as receiving nothing. The problem with leaving people out of your will altogether is that they may feel that you mistakenly forgot them, so much so that they may challenge your will. Instead, just list them in your will as receiving nothing. Your attorney will be able to use the correct language for this situation.

You can also leave them something small so that they are included in the will, but only by a fraction. Doing this will also serve to protect your will from those family members that seem to think they deserve something from your estate.

Monitoring Your Will throughout Your Life

You have heard the saying that life just happens. With a will, you need to make sure that when life happens, your will reflects what has happened to you. People get married, divorced, have kids, sell it all, invest it all, and even lose it all. As you go through your life, monitor what your will reflects to ensure that it provides for what you do want to happen when you are no longer alive.

The most important times to reassess your will include the times when your family makeup changes. For example, if you get married, everything changes to include your spouse. If you have a new child, you want to include him or her in your will as well. If you have a divorce, you want to go back and change the funds and property that you are giving your soon-to-be ex-wife or ex-husband. You will also want to look at your will for other reasons to make changes.

For example, if you have named a person in your will who dies before you, you should remove that person's name from the will and redirect the bequest. Otherwise, that person's heirs will stand in the shoes of that person to inherit under your will, which may not have been your intent. Even more important is to reassess your will if your spouse dies. Most people leave most or all their belongings to a spouse; if your spouse dies before you, you need to take this time to update your will to reflect the new need.

There may be events that happen in your life to make you change the way that you feel about those in your will. If you are considering a change because you want to pull someone out of your will, make sure that you are making the right decision. Take the time to seriously think about this decision. Additionally, you may be in need of changing your will because you lose a large amount of money, or you win the lottery.

Need to make a change?

If you do need to make a change to your will, the process is not that difficult. That means there is no excuse not to get this done.

There are two different methods to making this happen. The most straightforward way of changing your will is to completely rewrite it. Do not worry, as you are likely only making a few changes to the contents of the will. It is a matter of going into a file, making the changes, and printing a new document. Of course, you then must sign the new document, properly dated, in the presence of and with the signatures of two disinterested, competent witnesses, just as with your previous will. Your attorney will have this information on file for you, so the process can often take one meeting.

If you do not want to do this to your will and just want to make some minor changes or add a simple provision to it, then you can have your attorney draw up a codicil. This is a document that will accompany your will that makes changes. You should not attempt to write this document yourself because it must specifically reference portions of your will in legal format. Your attorney will need to prepare this document for you so that it will be legally binding.

You should go the route of a codicil if and when you want to only make minor changes, or when your competency at the time of executing the codicil may be challenged in some way.

In Virginia, because you have the option of a holographic will, you also have the option of changing your holographic will by writing out a new one or preparing a holographic codicil. If you do this, be sure to carefully date the new will and state you revoke all previous wills and sign your name. Also, remember a holographic will must be entirely in your handwriting, not partially typed or printed. If it is partially typed or printed, it is not holographic and must be witnessed with the formalities of other types of wills. If you write a holographic codicil to a will, it too must be entirely in your handwriting, signed, dated, and designated as a "codicil." Although holographic documents always carry the potential to raise questions and challenges, in some situations, they may be creatures of necessity, such as when there are no witnesses available in exigent circumstances. Where you have time to plan ahead and seek legal counsel — always the best approach — a holographic will or codicil is not necessary.

Also, while Virginia honors a holographic will, proving the will in probate requires two witnesses who can verify your handwriting. This suggests that after you have prepared your will and are satisfied with it, you should consider self-proving it with two witnesses attesting it as in your handwriting by your own statement, in the same way as a formally attested will is done.

Revoking your will

The most universal method to revoke your will is to write a new one that conforms to the will preparation laws of Virginia. Most states recognize certain acts as significant for revoking a will. Virginia describes acts of revocation acts as follows: "If a testator having an intent to revoke, or some person at his direction and in his presence, cuts, tears, burns, obliterates, cancels, or destroys a will or codicil, or the signature thereto, or some provision thereof, such will, codicil, or provision thereof is thereby void and of no effect."

Your Will's Status

You have done your part: You have written your will; you feel good about it and know that those whom you love the most will be taken care of.

All you can do now is keep your will up-to-date and make sure that it is legally sound. But you may be wondering what happens when you die. Now, we will dedicate a whole chapter to the world of probate, but before we do that, we want you to realize the process of your will's status.

There are three phases of your will's status. During this time, your will is being considered. Is this real? Is this what he wanted? Should what is written here be honored?

The status of your will when you die will fall into one of these categories:

- **Testacy**: This is where you want to be. In this status, your will is valid, and it has all it needs to be held up in court. If you die testate, that means that your will is valid in that your wishes are clearly defined throughout the document. Your wishes can be carried out, and you will die knowing that it is in good hands.
- **Intestacy**: If you die without a valid will, you die in intestate, which means that the legal system gets control of your estate and will determine who gets what. The laws of intestate succession are used to determine what happens to your estate. Laws in each state are somewhat different, but their basic standpoint is the same. They will take your estate and divide it among those who are considered to be your heirs. If you want funds to go to someone else who is not a relative of yours, then they are out of luck. Even worse, if you do not have any living relatives, the end result is that the state ends up with your estate.
- **Partial intestacy**: Here, you are someplace in the middle. You have a will, but there is something wrong with it. For some reason, it may not be legally binding, or there may be something that was left out of it. For example, if you did not include a residuary clause in your will, and you forgot to include something, there is no one to pass it on to. When you are in partial intestacy, once again, the state gets to decide who gets your property by using these laws. The best way to avoid this is to ensure that your attorney has made certain each part

of your will is binding and that the will is complete. This is another reason to hire a professional to handle your estate planning.

Planning your will is not nearly done. There are going to be other matters that you need to know along the way. For that, let us proceed to the next chapter.

Richmond, Virginia

Chapter 4

Laws That You Have to Deal With

Although will planning is about making peace with what will become of your property and doing whatever you want with it, there are also laws that must be followed. Sometimes, these laws can limit what you can do. Each law is intended to benefit a specific group of people, yet it is important for you to take into consideration how each one affects you.

Working with your attorney will help you to overcome some of the obstacles that you face in will planning. It is essential that you understand that some things are not as easy to plan as others are. Due to this, we have included the following information.

As mentioned in the previous chapter, like all states, Virginia has its own set of laws regarding wills. These laws affect not only what you can do in your will, but also how your estate plan will be carried out after you are gone. Understanding these laws can help you safeguard yourself, your property, and your heirs. Most of the time, setting up your property in a will can be enough to circumvent these laws so that they work in your favor.

There are two compelling motives behind advance estate planning — or, at least, there should be. One is a person's desire to have personal control and final decision over his or her belongings and take care of certain people they expect to leave behind. The other is to avoid the loss of a greater portion of the value of those belongings than absolutely necessary to taxes, court costs, and attorney or administrative fees. How estates are managed through the process of the probate courts and those aspects of estate planning that operate outside the probate process are the product of a legal orchestration of facts and circumstances in each individual case according to the restrictions and nuances of state law, with a few twists of federal tax law where applicable. The more advance planning a person does with the advice of a knowledgeable attorney and other members of the counseling team, the easier and more efficiently the estate will play out when the time comes for its distribution. Even so, there will be unforeseen events that make demands on your estate.

As you prepare your Virginia will, pay attention to these statutes and laws. You should have talked to your attorney about them and know how they affect your will and estate plan. Planning around and with them can make a difference in helping to protect you from the start.

Abatement Statutes and Laws

The most common of the various laws that will affect the outcome of your will are the abatement statutes. In simple terms, an abatement statute is in place to help figure out what to do when your estate is not worth what your will says it should be. Who will get what, now that there is not enough to give? You may think this is not going to be a problem, but it happens more than you may think. Costs, life emergencies, doctors' bills, or just unplanned expenses are in place often after a person passes on, and they may not be accounted for in the will.

There is also the problem that arises when people plan to have money to leave behind, but end up with debts that need to be paid instead. Abatement statutes help to define what should happen when you die and leave behind debt.

An abatement statute is the process of reducing or lessening something so that all parties can be equally paid as they should be. These laws do change from state to state, yet they all have one goal: to help determine who should get the available funds and how debts should be paid down.

Abatement statutes also define what happens in your estate first. For most cases, debts must be paid down within a certain time before the actual value of the estate can be shared among your family members. Breaking down these numbers and the order in which they will be paid is crucial. Sometimes, if you have residue in your estate plan, which means that there are extra funds in it, these funds may be reduced by abatement before the funds that are set aside to pay to your heirs as specific requests.

So, what can you do about these laws? First, you should know what they are. Work with your attorney specifically on this topic so that you can fully understand what is likely to happen should there be a need for an abatement statute to occur.

Then, plan for it. You can put language into your will that can help make your wishes known, as far as who should pay what. Most of the time, your attorney will be able to provide for specifics on how your assets will be used to pay off debt. You can also specify in what order your estate should be used to do this. Therefore, you still do have some say in how your money is used to pay down your debts and how abatement will affect your estate.

While this can seem confusing, it does not have to be. With the right language in your will, it can easily be spelled out. For example, if you want to leave your children an equal share of your estate, then you do not want to spell out exact dollars in your will. Instead, using language that says "equal parts" will help to work around abatements. If your estate was valued at $500,000, and you said in your estate plan that you wanted each of your five children to receive $100,000, this could be a potential problem. If your investments do not do as well as you think they will, there may be only $400,000 in your estate. Then, with this type of language, there is a problem, and abatement laws must be used to determine who gets what.

This same process can be used to help define what happens to debts that you owe. When the debts, such as medical expenses, credit card debt, or other debts, are paid, with the correct language in your will, your heirs still get to receive what you want them to.

Your will may not be worth what you had planned for in dollars and cents, but with the right language, your wishes can play out. After your debt is paid down, then you can distribute your funds and estate to your heirs the way that you want to. Unfortunately, it is difficult to do this in numbers, but in percentages, it works well. This way, you still determine the amounts that work for your wishes, but safeguard against abatements.

Paying off your debt

One common misconception is that when you die, your debts go with you. That is not the case, and there are going to be people, most often your heirs, who have to pay off what you owe. This tends to be done through your estate. We will learn more about this in Chapter 5; for now, you need to fully understand that you have to plan for debts that you may owe when you die. No matter how well you plan and how much you are valued at, you still need to take this into consideration, or someone else will have to deal with it.

In short, you plan for debts in your estate plan by realizing that you must factor them into determining the value of your estate. If you do not do this, you cannot have an accurate estimate of your estate's value. Even those who have good intentions of paying down all their debt need to figure it in, because, in the worst-case scenario, if you die tomorrow, it is there to be dealt with.

Abatement happens

No matter how well you have planned, it is possible there will be debts owed when you die that will exceed the value of some of your bequests. Your bequests are the property you leave to loved ones. Your debts must be paid before your bequests and the remaining residuary of your estate can be distributed to your beneficiaries named in the will. Unless you have directed in your will for such debts to be handled in a specific way, state law steps in to direct how the bills will be paid. This is called abatement of legacy.

The complexities arising from abatement to satisfy your creditors provide another illustration of the importance of using sage legal advice in setting up your will with advance estate planning. If there are specific types of property in particular that you want to shelter from creditors, or persons whose bequests you intend to have top priority in your will, then you must plan carefully how to account for these things ahead of time.

Antilapse Statutes

Another problem that must be handled is that of antilapse. Should someone in your will pass away before you do, there has to be some law in place to help determine what to do with that person's share of your estate. There are laws in place to fix this problem, as best that it can be, but it is also up to you to protect yourself against this type of situation.

If you do not make plans about how to handle this situation, then these statutes are in place to make those decisions. Yet you can circumvent those problems by naming a contingent beneficiary to your will. This person will be the catch-all for your estate. For example, you may leave your cousin James $20,000. But if he does not survive you, then if you have named your son as your contingent beneficiary, he would receive those funds.

Some states have antilapse laws, while others do not. Virginia does, as referenced in Virginia Code section 64.1-64.1. If beneficiary named in your will predeceases you, and you have not provided an alternative beneficiary, Virginia looks to the relationship of the beneficiary to you. If the deceased beneficiary was your grandparent or a direct descendant of a grandparent, then Virginia awards the bequest to the closest lineal descendant(s) of the deceased beneficiary. If you want to specifically say what happens to your estate should someone in your will pass away before you, get it written into your will through a contingent beneficiary.

Ademption Statutes

Yet another consideration is that of ademption. In ademption, there are laws in place that protect heirs who do not or cannot receive what you leave to them. If you, for some reason, include property in your will and estate to someone and that property is no longer part of your estate when you die, then there are laws that play a role in this situation.

For example, let us say that you leave your set of fine china to your daughter. But if you have sold the set prior to passing away to help pay down your medical debt, then that is no longer a piece of property that can be passed on to your daughter. The ademption clause and statutes will come into play in this case.

These laws vary from state to state, but ademption is something to consider planning for. Your heir may be able to claim the property if he or she can prove that you were not competent at the time the property was sold or given away. If this happens, your heir may have some ability to get those pieces of property, but this is hard to prove and difficult to make happen.

Another time when the ademption statutes come into play is when you have given your daughter that china already. While this is not a problem, assuming that the correct gift taxes are used, it still will be property that is considered in ademption because it is no longer part of your estate when you die. Any property that is not part of your estate when you die is considered to be adeemed, or unable to be divided. This also is the case for property which somehow ends up missing. Some states would consider the china "adeemed by satisfaction" and simply remove it from the estate. Virginia, though, makes no such assumption unless the testator has expressly stated so. Virginia Code section 64.1-63.1 states: "Property which a testator gave during his lifetime to a person shall not be treated as a satisfaction of a devise or bequest to that person, in whole or in part, unless (i) the will provides for deduction of the lifetime gift, (ii) the testator declares in a contemporaneous writing that the gift is to be deducted from the devise or bequest or is in satisfaction thereof, or (iii) the devisee or legatee acknowledges in writing that the gift is in satisfaction."

This statute underscores the importance of expressing your wishes ahead of time. If you include property in your will that is considered to be adeemed property, the ademption clause will be used to help determine what should happen, if anything can be done. It also helps to determine whether your heir should receive anything in the will. In addition, the statutes will say what that beneficiary can receive.

You should plan for this type of scenario with your attorney. Your attorney can help you determine the "what ifs" that are important in determining where your property will go. There can be additional language in your will to help protect you from this type of scenario, as well as what can remedy what will happen if you have property that cannot be included in your will because you are not in ownership of it any longer.

Advancement of Legacy

Another way a bequest in a will could be deemed satisfied in advance is if the testator conveyed it as a gift in advance during his or her lifetime to the legatee. This is called an advancement. Virginia Code section 64.1-63.1 expressly addresses how this has to work in Virginia:

> "Property which a testator gave during his lifetime to a person shall not be treated as a satisfaction of a devise or bequest to that person, in whole or in part, unless (i) the will provides for deduction of the lifetime gift, (ii) the testator declares in a contemporaneous writing that the gift is to be deducted from the devise or bequest or is in satisfaction thereof, or (iii) the devisee or legatee acknowledges in writing that the gift is in satisfaction."

This means that if you leave your nephew your Rolex watch in your will and decide to gift it to him in advance, you must amend your will to reflect the gift, or otherwise memorialize the gift in writing at the time you give it to him. At the very least, you should get a written receipt from him stating that it satisfies the legacy in your will. The latter might be something that happens in a deathbed situation. Otherwise, the nephew may be entitled to a monetary equivalent to the watch from the estate to satisfy the bequest even though he has already received the watch. Amending the will with a condici written by legal counsel is the best means, if possible.

Death and Divorce: Two Common Considerations

Divorce happens to one out of every two marriages — in other words, 50 percent of the time. Although you may not believe it could happen to you, divorce is a fact of life and should be planned for when creating your will.

The other situation most people do not want to think about is that of their spouse dying before they do. In cases like this, with no way to foretell if something unfortunate occurs, whatever your will says is supposed to cover the event.

It is important to realize that if you do not plan for one of these events and they end up happening, you will find your will is left open to what the laws governing wills dictate. Therefore, it is important to work closely with your attorney to determine what you can do and what you should do to protect yourself from these situations.

Divorce: Planning for it

Even if you are certain that your marriage will be successful, you still need to use your will to protect your other heirs from a potential divorce. If you do not plan for it in your will, you may not change your will right after the filing of divorce, and this can leave a possible problem should something happen to you.

Many people who do file for divorce do not make changes to their will right away and simply keep putting it off. When this happens, the risks are inevitable. Sometimes people do not want to make changes in their will because doing so would ultimately say that they are admitting that their marriage is over, or they may just forget to do so. In any case, not making changes can lead to mistakes.

Yet that is not always the case. Many of the states today have taken into account divorce. If there is a divorce, and changes have not been made in the will, there is still some protection for those that are left behind.

In Virginia, a will provision granting anything to a spouse is expressly revoked by statute once the marriage is divorced, dissolved, or annulled. If you have provisions for a spouse in your will and do nothing to change that, the fact of the divorce will have revoked them. If you wish to still leave anything to your ex-spouse in your will, you must make a new will, or when you make your will in the first place, you must state that he or she still inherits even if there is a legal separation, divorce, dissolution, or annulment. In Virginia, if spouses remarry after a divorce and the will was never changed, the will's provision for the spouse is revived. Again, this is not something to be handled without the advice and drafting assistance of legal counsel.

Death at the same time

Sometimes, death happens to both spouses at the same time, which can pose a real problem in will planning. Let us say that a husband and wife both die in the same fatal car accident. Unfortunately, doctors cannot determine who died first, and therefore, the will that they have designed for situations in which one of them dies before the other cannot be used. The end result is that they have to rely on the state's statutes regarding this type of situation to determine what happens to their will and their estate.

All states have some form of law that offers protection and understanding in situations like this. These laws are called the Uniform Simultaneous Death Act. This law is important to understand when there is a need to determine who died first. If your will has specific language in it that talks about surviving your spouse, which most wills will include if you are married, then this is an important statute to understand.

In most cases where there cannot be any assumption of who has died first in a simultaneous death, it is determined by these laws that you each survived the other. Virginia follows this rule under its Uniform Simultaneous Death Law — Virginia Code section 64.1-104 — which states that a person must survive the other by 120 hours, as proved by clear and convincing evidence. Otherwise, they are deemed to have died simultaneously.

Each will and estate plan is executed assuming that you survived your spouse. This ensures that your property is divided the way in which your will specifies assuming you lived longer than your spouse.

In most cases, this is good news because it allows your estate to avoid going through probate twice. In addition, it can save you money in estate costs. Yet if these are not your wishes, then it becomes a problem that you need to address beforehand. To protect yourself from such problems, you should include a survival clause in your will. This will make the necessary provisions for a simultaneous death situation based on the best and most profitable method according to what you and your attorney determine.

This is important in cases when you do not die at the same time, but within a short time of one another. If one spouse is injured and dies days after the other, the possible problem here is that the estate will end up passing through estate probate twice because the will of the first to die will go into effect, passing the estate to the other. When you use a survival clause, you are able to sidestep this process. Should the person who receives your estate die within a certain amount of time after you do, you will void that part of your will, and the estate will pass to the other beneficiaries that you have determined. This keeps your estate out of probate for at least one round. You can add language into your will that says that the beneficiary must survive 30, 60, or some other number of days after you to receive your will's specifications.

Each of these situations shows you how you will need to handle the planning of your estate in cases where laws are in place that can alter what your wishes happen to be. It is important to make these changes in your will so that you can avoid possible problems later.

Not all laws and statutes can be changed by your will, as we have shown you. There are a handful of laws that you will have to deal with when creating your will that cannot be sidestepped or overcome easily.

Sometimes Laws Get in the Way No Matter What

Sometimes, there are laws that states have on the books that you just cannot overlook or somehow get around. These laws are part of the building process of a will — something you need to learn about. Even if you do not like what you see, it is what the law dictates, and even if you include language in your estate that says that you do not want this to happen, it still may.

Here, we will go through some of the various laws that could affect the outcome of your will and estate. Each state has different laws that need to be taken into consideration. We will point out Virginia's position.

In some cases, these laws are in place to protect your heirs if you are being malicious or otherwise causing them financial harm by trying to leave them nothing in your will. The state will then determine whether the will should be honored and otherwise provide for your heirs. Many people try to include such things in their will and spend thousands of dollars trying to make it happen — only to find out that probate changes everything anyway. Therefore, understanding these laws will save you time and money in the long run. If you do not want your will to be voided, you need to understand these statutes and laws fully.

Community property stipulations

There are some laws that protect community property, or property that is shared between you and your spouse. But it is not just your home that is being referred to here. Any money made or anything in ownership or acquired during your community property state of living is divided equally between the spouses. Therefore, if you die while living in a community property state, at least 50 percent of what you own will be left to your spouse because it is their property as well.

Not all states have this — the following do:

- Arizona
- California
- Idaho
- Louisiana
- Nevada
- New Mexico
- Texas
- Washington
- Wisconsin (Marital property instead of community property)

In these states, you are required to leave your spouse 50 percent of what you own, and that includes anything that has been purchased or acquired in virtually any legal way during your marriage. The only type of property that you can completely call your own is any gift or inheritance that was received by you personally and solely. The only other property that may qualify is property that you owned prior to getting married — and you can show that you have owned it for that amount of time. Yet even this is subject to determination by probate.

If your sole property becomes community property, which is something that can happen if you place funds or other property with what you both own, then it can be considered the same as community property. Therefore, if you have this type of property and you do not want to it fall under this realm, keep it separate in some way. If this applies to you, it is suggested that you discuss this subject with your attorney in order to ensure your wishes are carried out properly.

Those states that do not have this law often have other laws that dictate how much of your estate is yours.

Common law states

The other states, including Virginia, all have what is called common law in regard to property ownership in a marriage. In Virginia, you do still have to divide the property between the two of you, but it is not necessarily an equal share as it is in a community property state. The division of property is determined through the spousal elective shares law that the state has in place in which your spouse can say that he or she has a claim to some of your property. The amount of your estate that your spouse can claim is determined by these laws. Each state offers a different determination on what that is, though. Work with your attorney to determine this.

Note, though, that Virginia expressly recognizes the community property laws of other states as to property owned in those states by Virginia residents. To the extent this may be the case, your Virginia estate will be further complicated by the community property laws of those states affecting the distribution of that property under your Virginia will or trust.

If you have wishes as far as where your property goes and want to provide for that in your will, you can, but that does not mean it has to be honored. It is up to your spouse to determine what they want. If you provide for more than what the state's elective shares does, then your spouse can accept that amount. But, if you try to provide them with less than this amount, then your spouse does not have to accept that amount and can go for the higher number as defined by law.

Again, when your estate's value changes, your estate must be handled by law in determining who gets what and where it all goes. You should never try to leave your spouse less than what Virginia's elective shares law requires, or you may have less say in what happens to your money.

You cannot sidestep these measures. For example, if you try to by moving property around before you die so that your spouse cannot include it in the value of the estate, this can be something that is placed back into the value of the estate, should it be deemed possible. These laws are in place to protect the surviving spouse from your efforts to limit what they can claim as their own.

Let us say that you know you are dying and therefore move your property into your son's name. You are hoping that your property does not fall claim to your spouse's rights to that property. However, if you die within a certain amount of time after doing this type of transfer, the value of that property transfer can be added back into your estate, and your beneficiaries cannot claim it. This is called an augmented estate.

If there are problems in your marriage and you do not want to leave your spouse anything, you should consider filing for divorce, which can provide you with more protection. Although you may not realize it, all your hard work in keeping your spouse from getting your property may be useless when the state sees what you are doing. Try to handle anything like this before you die so that you do not leave your estate and beneficiaries in the hole later.

Protecting your homestead through your will

There are a handful of states that provide a homestead law, which allows you to help protect your family by maintaining your homestead or an equivalent subsidy. Virginia's homestead law is discussed below, and possibly may not be considered adequate for your needs.

The will is set up to help maintain this property and therefore is an excellent consideration, especially when you have quite a bit of land. If you have a spouse and/or minor children, this may also be an ideal way to make sure they have a home for some time after your death. If you owe money and have this stipulation in your will, it helps to protect the home from being taken to pay the debt. But it is not a sure thing.

This type of law helps give your family some time to find ways to pay the debt, perhaps by selling something. Doing this helps prevent creditors from taking the home from your family immediately. It does not mean, though, that creditors cannot force the sale of a home, because if not enough money can be found, this may be necessary. Nevertheless, it could buy them some time.

While most of your intangible personal property, such as your cash, cannot be kept away from creditors who have valid claims against your estate, sometimes your tangible property can be. That means that you can find value in a protective clause that allows your family to keep some of this type of property. Virginia provides for homestead, family allowance, and certain exempt property.

Family allowance laws protect your family

There are many problems that families experience when the main financial provider dies. If you are the one whom your family relies on to pay the bills, you may believe that your family can use whatever you have given them to keep on paying the bills and doing what they need to in order to keep themselves safe if you die. Yet what you may not realize is that probate takes a long time to go through. Until it does, your family may be without anything from you.

First, you want to plan for situations in which your family will receive as much support as possible should you die. You need to consider when those funds will be available to your family.

If you wish to make sure your family is protected upon your death, do not just include your wishes in a will. Instead, you need to make sure that your family is given what is called a family allowance until probate can be settled. It can take a year or more for that to happen in some states, including Virginia. If a mortgage payment is missed for just two or three months (often just two), they already risk losing their home.

Family allowance in Virginia

A family allowance is just what it sounds like, and it is a near-immediate tool that you have available to you. If your estate enters probate without this type of statute in place in your will, your family cannot tap into the funds that you have allocated to them until all your debts have been paid in full, which can take some time. A family allowance, though, can be paid out during this time to help keep the family living in the same manner that they need to.

But how much they get is another story. You see, there is an important consideration that each estate must go through. How much your family can receive is determined by how much your family's expenses are, as well as what your estate's value is.

Virginia Code section 64.1-151.1 provides for a family allowance during the pendency of the estate's administration, as follows:

> "Upon the death of a domiciliary [resident] of this Commonwealth [of Virginia], the surviving spouse and minor children whom the decedent was obligated to support are entitled to a reasonable allowance in money out of the estate for their maintenance during the period of administration, which allowance may not continue for longer than one year if the estate is inadequate to discharge all allowed claims. The family allowance may be paid as a lump sum in one or more installments or in periodic installments. It is payable to the surviving spouse, if living, for the use of the surviving spouse and minor children, otherwise, to the person having the care and custody of the minor children; but in case any minor child is not living with the surviving spouse, the family allowance may be made partially to the spouse and partially to the person having the child's care and custody as their needs may appear. If there are no minor children, the allowance is payable to the surviving spouse. The family allowance has priority over all claims against the estate.
>
> The family allowance is in addition to any benefit or share passing to the surviving spouse or minor children by the will of the decedent, by intestate succession, or by way of elective share. The death of any person entitled to family allowance terminates the person's right to any allowance not yet paid."

Note three factors especially important about this statute: (1) the allowance is in addition to any other entitlement the spouse and children may have coming to them under the will or the law; (2) it will last up to a year; (3) the amount, whether paid in lump sum or periodically, is that which the court deems "reasonable" under the circumstances.

You should closely work with your attorney to determine what this allowance is likely to be. An estate planning attorney will be able to help you plan for just how much your family is likely to receive. If you do not feel that it will be enough, and your family will need additional income to make it through this time, you will want to consider setting up a separate gift-giving strategy that will provide funds to your beneficiaries. This can be a valuable tool for protecting your family. Such strategies can be discussed with your estate attorney and planning team to ensure your family is protected after your death.

Surviving family's right to exempt property in Virginia

Under Virginia Code section 64.1-151.2, in addition to the family allowance described above, there is certain "exempt property" that the surviving spouse (or minor children if there is no surviving spouse) is entitled to have out of the estate in a value not to exceed $15,000, exclusive of any liens on the property. This property is listed in the statute as: "household furniture, automobiles, furnishings, appliances, and personal effects."

What if the listed types of exempt property are insufficient to equal $15,000? The statute has an answer to this. "[I]f there is not $15,000 worth of exempt property in the estate, the spouse or minor children are entitled to other assets of the estate, if any, to the extent necessary to make up the $15,000 value. Rights to exempt property and assets needed to make up a deficiency of exempt property have priority over all claims against the estate, but not over the family allowance."

This language serves to provide additional protection for the surviving spouse, as it is combined with the family allowance, but also suggests possible limitations on specific bequests of property you might list in your will, depending on what will be designated as falling within the $15,000 exempt property group within the estate, or whether the exempt property will be inadequate. Clearly you want to discuss the impact of this provision on your estate with your estate planning Virginia lawyer.

Virginia homestead allowance

In addition to the family allowance and exempt property provision, Virginia provides a homestead allowance for surviving spouse (or minor children if no surviving spouse) under certain circumstances. Virginia Code section 64.1-151.3 explains how the homestead allowance works, as follows:

> "In addition to the right to family allowance and exempt property, a surviving spouse of a decedent who was domiciled in this Commonwealth [of Virginia] is entitled to a homestead allowance of $15,000. If there is no surviving spouse, each minor child of the decedent is entitled to a homestead allowance amounting to $15,000, divided by the number of minor children of the decedent. The homestead allowance has priority over all claims against the estate, but not over the right to family allowance and exempt property.
>
> The homestead allowance is in lieu of any share passing to the surviving spouse or minor children by the will of the decedent or by intestate succession; provided, however, if the amount passing to the surviving spouse and minor children by the will of the decedent or by intestate succession is less than $15,000, then the surviving spouse or minor children shall be entitled to a homestead allowance in an amount which, when added to the property passing to the surviving spouse and minor children by the will of the decedent or by intestate succession, will equal the sum of $15,000."

The language of the homestead allowance statute indicates its intent is a contingency to ensure there is $15,000 provision made if other provisions of the will fail to meet that number. In addition, if the surviving spouse takes an elective share allowed by Virginia law, then the homestead allowance is not available to the surviving spouse. Still, the homestead provision is clearly stated to be "in addition to" the family allowance and exempt property provisions of Virginia's Code.

Be sure you understand how all three of these provisions affect your Virginia estate planning. A Virginia legal specialist is the best person to advise you.

Those not in your will...yet

Suppose you have a newborn child and you do not update your will before you die. Most states have laws that provide for some protection so that your family members can be protected, even when you may not have included them in the will. These are called pretermitted or omitted heir statutes and vary from state to state. They always only include your spouse and your children, though. Should you die before you can include them in your will, there are stipulations that allow you to give them something. States mandate, in some cases, that these individuals be given something. Virginia picks up where the will is silent. It is presumed that the testator would have provided for the pretermitted heir, had he or she been aware of the heir.

As you have seen, laws can help you during the process of setting up your will, but they can also play a problematic role. Most laws do have good intentions; they just may not be your intentions. You should work closely with your estate planning attorney to find out what you can do in Virginia to make sure that your wishes are fully carried out, under the letter of the law, as much as you can. Do not assume that you can do anything you want in your will; learn for certain what you can and cannot do so that you do not waste your time.

Robert E. Lee's Mansion, Arlington, Virginia

Chapter 5

Probate: Avoid It at All Costs

If you know what probate is, you know that you want to avoid it. But do you know what it means and how it works? It costs quite a bit of money and is a long, time-consuming process. If you can, avoid it by having a good plan for your estate (something you are doing well at right now by reading this book).

Understanding probate is important because many estates pass through this process. Probate can mean the presenting of a will to a court official so that it can be filed, but it is more commonly a term that is used to describe the process of going through the settling of a will. The process of probate is a long one, but one that happens to many. Here is a brief look at what the process involves:

- Filing the will with the court, usually done by the estate's attorney.
- Determining and inventorying the deceased person's property and estate.

- Determining the need for and having an appraisal of the property done.

- Paying off any money that is owed in taxes or otherwise through the estate, such as paying off debts.

- The will must be "proved valid," which means that the court rules that the document filed is a legitimate will. In 90 percent of the cases, this is done as a routine matter, unless someone has a valid reason to contest the will.

- Giving notice of the will to the deceased heirs, i.e. those who would have a valid claim on the estate if there was no will.

- Finally, the estate is distributed to those that are listed in the will.

If you do not have a will or any other legal means to distribute your property, your estate still must go through probate. If your will is found to be invalid, then the estate will go through probate "intestate," i.e., without a will.

If a will or an estate has to go through probate, the end result is likely to be a large waste of money and time. Most of the time, there is no need for there to be any lengthy, extensive process. There tends to be no one saying that the will is not valid, and in most cases, the estate will be divided by those that are left behind anyway, so there is no reason to worry about this.

Should your estate enter probate, it will likely go through the process for at least one full year. During this time, creditors and others who feel they have a stake in the estate have the right to come forward and say so. Any creditor who does not do so in the amount of time allotted by Virginia's laws will not be able to collect against the estate once it has filed. Probate is by far one of the most drawn-out legal issues facing people today. If you were to establish a living trust — which we will soon discuss in detail in Chapter 7 — instead of a will to dole out your property, you could complete the process in a matter of just weeks, rather than a full year.

During the probate process, there is a need to have someone who can legally get through the system to help you. You will hire a probate lawyer to handle the process. This person will work toward closing the case, but it means a making a few court appearances as well as filling out some paperwork. Your estate planning attorney should be able to do this for you, but make sure he or she is all right with helping you get through the process much faster if possible.

You will also have named an executor or executrix in your will. This is most often a member of your family or close friend in whom you have entrusted the job of carrying out your wishes as you have stated them in your will. If for some reason the person you name cannot serve — nor can any backup person you name — the court will appoint an administrator for the will, just as it appoints someone to administer your estate if you die intestate — or without a will. The administrator is entitled to payment of fees for these services. In Virginia, the court determines reasonable fees to be paid. The executor or administrator follows the lead of the attorney for the estate, but still has fiduciary obligations to discharge and carries legal obligations reportable to the court. The executor or administrator fees, unless the person waives them, are charged against the estate's assets as a cost.

The Cost of Probate

One of the hottest issues with those who have to work through the probate system is its cost. Many expenses are tacked on during this process. Many times, the largest costs are the attorneys themselves.

Each state has different laws in regard to what attorneys can charge in probate cases. This amount changes based on location; for example, if you live in California, you can expect to pay more than someone living in Wyoming. Yet each state's laws are different in how they figure out this amount as well. In some states, like Virginia, as long as the Court determines that a fee for a probate attorney is "reasonable," it can be charged. In other states, a percentage system is used instead. That means that the attorney receives a percentage of what the estate is valued at.

There are other fees as well. Legally, the executor of the will is entitled to a fee for their services, which is determined by the court or statute. Because in most cases the estate's executor is also a beneficiary of the will, executors often refuse payment. Yet it is still his or her legal right to accept it.

Another set of fees comes from the actual legal system. There are court costs and fees for having the property appraised that can run you several hundred dollars or more. You will find that there are additional fees for filing the paperwork or having a notary sign the paper you must file.

Is it necessary to have a probate attorney?

One way to cut out the costs of an attorney is to have the executor do the court appearances himself. While this sounds like a good solution, and one that could be pulled off by most, a few states do not allow it. In other states, judges make it difficult for the executors, which makes them even less effective.

Two states, California and Wisconsin, have a system in place that will allow this. It is called the in pro per action procedure, which is something that those living in those locations can look into. This simply means that the executor can stand "in pro per," or represent your estate her- or himself without the help of an attorney. These states have procedures in place to help individuals do this.

On the other hand, those states that do not have these specific procedures in place but do not have any laws against the process, including Virginia, are nearly impossible to benefit from. There are intricate details that need to be completed, and there is not much help for those who are not legally educated. If you do not have a lawyer through the process, you will not get much help from judges or other court-appointed individuals, which will lengthen the procedure.

In Virginia, you do not necessarily have to have an attorney to help you through the probate process. While this may be the case, the executor will need to either thoroughly educate her- or himself by visiting a library, getting some help from law books, or having someone else help.

There are also court costs involved in probating a will. Virginia courts have specific fees associated with the filing of various forms and actions connected with requirements, beginning with the filing of the initial probate action. Depending upon the items in the estate requiring attention of the court — for example, appointment of appraisers, will contests, or hearings — these fees can add up quickly. Copies of papers authorizing the executor or administrator to take action on behalf of the estate come at a cost. Such copies are important to be able to obtain information from banks and communicate with taxing authorities, just to name two areas where such identification is important.

Avoid It if Possible

Although skipping the attorney seems like a good option for saving money, it is still risky and difficult. Instead, see whether you can at least avoid probate for some of your larger estate pieces and therefore cut the costs considerably. Avoiding probate, if possible, is the best solution for those looking for reduced fees.

If you have the opportunity to do so, transferring as much of your property as possible out of your will into another means to get it to those whom you love may be one of the best things you can do. It can save you thousands of dollars because most of the other options for leaving your belongings behind to your heirs do not have to go through probate.

To help you make that decision, consider these different types of tools to help you to move your property and estate from your possession into the possession of others.

In Virginia, you may consider several alternatives or a combination of them, depending on your circumstances. This is where your estate planning team comes into play for you. Alternatives include: life insurance policies or trusts; transfer or payable-on-death accounts in banks or similar institutions such as investment companies; securities; gifting assets before you die; use of retirement plan accounts; revocable living trusts; AB trusts; a joint tenancy with right of survivorship; and a tenancy in common.

Joint tenancy with survivorship

Joint tenancy with survivorship is a commonly used vehicle to pass real estate in Virginia outside of probate. It is most often used by married couples, but is not limited to them. It can be set up by people who own property together. If you set up a joint tenancy with survivorship deed to real property with more people on the deed than just your spouse, be aware that your spouse's interest will not expire if you divorce. As with all legal instruments, you are well-advised to obtain the assistance of an attorney knowledgeable about real property deeds and estate planning when you contemplate entering into a joint tenancy survivorship arrangement. You want to be sure you have the deed correctly written and understand any tax ramifications, as well as rights to use of the property, order of distribution with each person's death, and other issues.

Tenancy by the entireties

Tenancy by the entireties is a concept not recognized in all states. Similar to joint tenancy with survivorship, this vehicle permits spouses only to own joint interest in real estate with survivorship rights that are immune from creditors of one of the co-owners. Virginia law so far recognizes tenancy by the entireties.

Living trust

Another mechanism is a living trust. This tool avoids probate completely and gives you quite a bit of control over your property as you age. You have a good amount of flexibility and are protected even in the event that you become incapacitated. Therefore, it is a safe, flexible option for transferring your estate to your heirs.

On the downside, a living trust can pose other kinds of problems. For example, it is more difficult to create. You will need to work with your estate planning attorney to plan out a thorough plan of action. You may find that this additional step does tack on some financial expense, but again, it can be money that is well invested. You will also have to maintain your living trust with your estate planning attorney over time. Living trusts do need to be updated and monitored for necessary changes, both in your circumstances and changes in the law.

Item-specific solutions

There are a few other solutions to consider as well. For example, you can use a transfer-on-death car registration in Virginia by a TOD joint ownership arrangement.

If you own bank accounts, IRAs, securities, or something similar, you can use a transfer-on-death or pay-on-death (POD) option to help move them from one owner to the next outside probate. It is an affordable, easy way to avoid probate. The only state that does not allow for them is Texas.

As with all such mechanisms, consultation with your estate planning team is advisable to orchestrate all these mechanisms if you have several options or alternatives under consideration.

Setting up a beneficiary account

If you have a pension plan, you can have a beneficiary named to that plan, which will pay directly to your beneficiary on your death. This will allow you to avoid probate of your income and keep your family taken care of relatively quickly. Make sure that you read through the details of these accounts, though, to find out whether there are any limits on what can and cannot be provided for in these situations.

You can also do this with your retirement accounts. By naming a beneficiary, you sidestep the probate system completely.

Once again, if you want to provide funds for your family that are easily accessible and quickly available to them, take out a life insurance policy. These are excellent vehicles for fast financial help, and proceeds from these policies are not allowed to go through probate. If you can afford it, it is well-worth it.

Other solutions

As mentioned, another consideration is pay-on-death (POD) bank accounts. These are an ideal option because they are not expensive to set up, and they avoid probate. It is a solution for those who have cash or securities to be distributed to adults.

These solutions work for many people because they offer the ability to get around the probate system, which is something that makes sense for most. Yet, there is much more to learn about how to avoid probate, but it is worth learning about.

Informally probating yourself

If you do not have many reasons for going through probate, such as having many assets, it can be possible to avoid probate. For example, if you do not have any debt and have only household items to your name, then when you die, your family can come to the home and divide up your belongings without any problem. In this case, there would not be any problem avoiding probate because there is no debt and there is little valuable property.

The only way for this to work is if:

- There is little property that belongs to the individual;
- The family is able to gain access to all the property of the individual;
- The family agrees on how the property will be divided up evenly;
- The family pays any and all creditors, without any problems regarding who will do this.

Simply stated, there is little or nothing to probate. Informal means like this can be easy to use. If you already know that you would like several people in your family to have certain items, you can make sure they receive them by talking with your family about your wishes and making sure they will honor this. Keep in mind that ultimately you will not control what they really do. There is not a legal way of dictating this or being 100-percent sure that it will go through as you would like it.

There are many types of property, though, that cannot go through this type of process. For example, if there is any real estate involved, it is not possible for you to informally let people just take it over unless you utilize the predetermined joint survivorship deed option mentioned above. There must be a legal authority who can say where the property will be transferred, not just a say-so from one of your heirs. If you have other items, like anything with a title, then these too cannot go through an informal means. These items require that a legal title change names, which means that lawyers do have to get involved.

The other problem that occurs with an attempt for informal avoidance of probate is that people often do not agree. If your son wants the living room furniture in your home and so does your daughter, and there is no way to come to an agreement about how property will be divided, the unhappy party has the right and the ability to file a formal probate, in which case the probate process begins, and the costs and the entire process of splitting up the property goes through the process as determined by Virginia law. The unhappy party is still unlikely to gain much due to probate costs.

The solution for you is to have a simple will that does not include much property and does not have any type of property that has a title attached to it. In this situation, your wishes must be followed as you define in your will, which will effectively eliminate the problems.

If creditors are not paid off in full, they too can file a formal probate, which would mean that the process of probate can happen so that every element of your property must be taken through the probate process. Therefore, heirs should pay down any and all creditors as much as possible, or you can prepare to leave some funds behind in savings to pay off creditors.

For most, planning to avoid probate means taking a long look at what they need to accomplish. If you are looking to take care of your children, you may not need to worry about planning to avoid probate just yet. Right now, the most important thing for you to do is to set up the means to care for your family. But if you are aging, now is the time to consider any of the methods that we have talked about to avoid probate. In the next chapter, we will go into more detail on how to avoid probate through other means.

Can Probate Be a Good Thing?

There are some times when probate can be a good thing for your heirs, such as if you have a large amount of debt. Often, this is the best way for what you owe to be settled.

If you have debts that exceed what would be considered normal, everyday household costs, you may not want to avoid probate.

Those who only have:

- Mortgages;
- Car or other vehicle payments;
- Credit card debt;
- Small debts such as subscriptions;

or

- Utility bills

. . . *do not* want to file probate.

Those who have:

- Debts that are larger from a business;

- A failed business;
- Large amounts owed to creditors that they know will come after their home;

or

- Pending lawsuits or claims against them

. . . *do* want to file probate, especially if their executors plan to fight those claims. Here, probate can help resolve creditor liability and can handle the legal action that many creditors will use to try to get their slice of the estate pie.

When you die with this type of debt being owed, the creditors have a limited amount of time to let their wishes be known. Sometimes this is as short as four months, sometimes as long as a year. If they do not speak up about their claim on your estate during that time, they lose their rights. But if they do, then your heirs may need probate to help them get through the process. In Virginia, creditors have at least six months after the personal representative of the estate is officially appointed by the court. There is some reference in the Virginia Code, though, to some cases where a creditor could assert a claim up to five years after an estate is distributed and closed. While this seems extreme, the reference underscores the importance of legal expertise in estate probate management if there are likely to be several creditors.

In addition, if there is any way that you think your estate will be challenged by anyone, then probate can be a benefit. For those who know there will be a challenge, probate is a solution because of just how hard it is for the challenger to win their case. They must show that somehow you have violated laws and therefore should be made to pay them some sort of money through your estate. They may have to prove that you were incompetent and unable to handle this type of decision-making process.

Unless these challengers can attack your will with a legally justified, provable reason that your will should not go through, they will not be given much leeway by judges. But if you do not allow the estate to go through probate, their time is longer for making claims against the estate, and they can fight your heirs legally for years about the will and the assets that you have. Therefore, allowing these situations to go through to probate is essential.

What is good and bad about probate?

Let us take one more look at the good side and the bad side of probate.

- Probate allows your estate to be divided fairly among your heirs as dictated by Virginia's laws.
- Probate has definite, defined procedures that help to protect you from attacks against your will by creditors or those claiming that your will is not valid.
- Probate helps to provide a transfer of your property that is fair and done correctly, as your will and laws dictate.
- Probate can be more costly than it should be if an attorney is used.
- Probate can be a long, drawn-out process that will not provide funds to your heirs quickly unless an allowance is permitted for day-to-day living expenses.

We will assume that you do not want your estate to go through probate because, although mentioned last, the final two points above are important points for you. Therefore, our recommendation is simple: Protect your assets that are worth any type of real value through another means if possible. In addition, have a backup will that dictates where everything will go and how it is to be handled. Your backup will can be used alongside, or at least as a backup plan, to your estate.

By creating a backup plan for your estate, you can protect your heirs and get them through an otherwise messy, costly proceeding.

Chapter 6

Will Substitutions That Can Conserve Your Estate

A will is only one option that you have for ensuring your estate goes where you want it to. It is, by far, the most commonly used tool to help you make decisions regarding your estate, but does not mean that it is the best or only option for you. There are a handful of products, like will substitutions, that can do a better job of protecting you and ensuring you do not have to go through probate. But which, if any, of these is the right product for your needs?

We will go through a set of different types of tools and the frequency with which they are used. You should look at several of them and work with your set of power players to make the right decisions. Your attorney, your tax advisor, and your financial planner are key to helping you overcome any possible problem with any of these solutions.

There are many benefits to using will substitutes. For starters, they give you more control over what happens to your estate. For example, you may be able to have more leeway on who gets what, even though Virginia law says something different. In some of these substitutions, you will also be able to override what your will says, making will substitutes the prime tool for determining what happens to your estate.

There are many reasons why you might want to override your will, but for the sake of time, let us give an example. Let us say that you write your will to include various elements that are important to you, but you do not have the ability to control your will as much as you would like to due to Virginia law, or perhaps you want to try to avoid probate. Therefore, your will is your backup plan. It may not be exactly what you want, but it is what is in place if everything else falls through.

In addition to your will, you may provide a living trust or another of the tools we will mention. Now, your will is overridden — assuming that is included in the language — and your living trust is in place. But should something go wrong there, the will would then hold its own ground. As you can see, this legal maneuvering can be complicated, but with the help of your attorney, it can be simplified.

When to Consider Substitutes

Here are a number of times and reasons why you may choose to consider will substitutes.

1. **You do not want to waste time.** You know that probate is a lengthy process, and if you know your family will need your estate faster than what probate can provide for them, you can establish a means for taking care of them while probate is happening, or even in lieu of it. With several of the will substitutes, property is transferred right away.

2. **You do not want to waste your money.** The cost of a probate attorney alone is reason enough to seek out additional help from these

substitutions. There are other laws in place that can be costly to you as well and can be avoided with the help of substitutions for the will. In Chapter 8, we will talk about new laws that are in place that seem to want to take quite a bit from your estate. But when filing a substitution for your will, the federal government cannot touch these pieces of your estate, and therefore you are protected.

3. **You want more control.** Many will substitutions allow you more control over what happens to your estate. As we mentioned, you get more say in what happens to your property when you use these tools.

Working with your team of advisors is the best way to determine what tools to use. Special circumstances can often help determine the right course of action for your needs.

Which Will Substitute Should You Consider?

There are several types of will substitutes that you can use. Some are well-worth your time, depending on what you need to use them for. To help you, let us break down some of the options that may be right for you.

Your options include: joint tenancy with survivorship, living trusts, tenancy by the entirety, payable-on-death accounts, life insurance, and other beneficiary accounts. Each fits a specific situation and should be used if you determine it is the best method.

What is Joint Tenancy with Survivorship?

Joint tenancy with right of survivorship is just what it sounds like. In Virginia, if you have this type of property ownership, both you and others own it equally. Each person owns the property in undivided equal value.

The key element of joint tenancy with survivorship is that when you die, the others who own the property with you on the deed continue to equally own the property among them as your survivors. Usually this is just one other person — your spouse — because married couples or domestic partners most often make use of this mechanism.

There are some roadblocks we will talk about shortly, but know that joint tenancy often works well for those who share property. Family members often do this so that when an elder dies, the property is kept in the family.

With this type of arrangement, the joint tenants who have survivorship rights are those who will be equally held as owners of the property; therefore, if one dies, the other gets the remaining property. But if one of the owners deeds his or her share of the property to someone else, that new person does not have rights of survivorship and will not get sole ownership of the home.

For example, let us say that you own a home with your spouse and have survivorship rights under joint tenancy. If you die, your spouse gets the remaining part of your home as his or her own in its entirety. But let us say, theoretically, that you instead decide to give your share of the home to your daughter through a deed. Now she owns your share, but she does not have survivorship rights. Therefore, if she dies before your spouse does, her heirs would get her share of the property, not your spouse. In other words, when you transferred your share, you changed the survivorship mechanism of the deed that takes the property outside of probate.

There are some benefits that can come of using joint tenancy over other types of will substitutions:

- **You will save money.** It is fast, easy, and inexpensive to set up a joint tenancy. Technically, you do not need an attorney to help you through the process, although having your estate planning attorney help you to determine the right course of action can be a positive thing. There is no attorney needed when the joint tenancy comes into play when someone dies, either.

- **It is easy for the transfer of the title to happen.** The process is simple and straightforward, with no question about whom the property goes to. If one of the joint tenants who has rights dies, then the other gets their share of the property. This can be helpful to many people who want to ensure that their property goes to one or several people specifically.

- **Debts that you have may be reduced.** If you have debts when you die, it is up to your estate representative to pay off those debts before your estate can be closed through probate. As you have learned, though, probate is a long process in which creditors must show that they have a stake in the property. If you own property and there is not enough cash to pay off the debts you owe, your representatives may need to sell property in order to pay creditors off. But joint tenancy property is not included in this most of the time. That is because this type of property is not part of probate and therefore not subject to the debt. But it is important to note that if you have selected to use joint tenancy to hide from the debts that you owe — and this can be proved — then your property can be considered part of the repayment plan.

Yet even with these benefits, there are some definite drawbacks to this type of will substitution that you must know about if you are to find success using it. Working with your attorney, you can clearly find out whether this is the right choice for you. But let us talk about some of the possible reasons why this may not be the best solution for you.

One of the greatest disadvantages of joint tenancy is the fact that you cannot leave your property to someone else after you have the joint tenancy in place. If you want the other joint tenant or tenancy to share your property with you, and you have no intention of wanting anyone else to have any share in it, then this is not a problem. But if you do want someone else to share in it, this is not the route to take.

If you end up being the sole survivor of the joint tenancy, you no longer have any survivors to pass that property down to. Therefore, you must make the decision to do something with the property or set up another joint tenancy with others who will get their share of the property should you die.

When you die, you no longer have any say in what happens to the property. Even if the other survivor has agreed to various stipulations as to what will happen to ownership of the property, you have no way of enforcing that, as it is completely their decision to do with the property as they see fit.

There are a few tax disadvantages as well. You should consult your tax advisor to fully understand what the tax benefits and disadvantages are in this type of will substitute. Should you have a stepped-up tax basis, then you could be paying quite a bit more for your joint tenancy than you thought. This could be a crucial decision in your outlook for tax planning during estate planning.

If you are not quite sure whether a joint tenancy is the right decision for you, work with your tax advisor and your estate planning attorney to determine the pros and cons for your specific case. You can also consider the other types of will substitutions.

What is a Living Trust?

Another solution to avoiding the use of a will for your estate needs is to use a living trust. While we will dedicate Chapter 7 to how to set one up and how to properly use it in your estate plan, a living trust is a popular choice for those who are considering a will substitution and therefore is briefly noted here.

A living trust is created while you are still alive and, therefore, is put in place prior to your death. What goes into this trust (called the trust principle)? First, a living trust is revocable during your lifetime. You remain in control of the trust assets and can manage the trust for yourself as its trustee while you are alive. You can change it or revoke (dissolve) it.

Another term for this type of trust is "revocable inter vivos trust." You are the recipient of the trust's proceeds during your lifetime. At any time before you die, you can make changes to your trust, or until the trust becomes irrevocable, such as if you were to become incapacitated. After your death, the trust principle is distributed to the beneficiaries you designate in the trust.

Who is important to know?

There are several key people in the living trust, each with their own role and responsibility in making your wishes come true. Let us go through them, one by one, and find out how a trust works.

The trustor, or grantor, is you, the creator of the trust. The trustee is the person who legally manages the trust for the income beneficiaries. You may be the trustee and be the sole income beneficiary. The income beneficiaries are those who receive income from the trust during your lifetime. The remainder beneficiaries are those who receive what is left in the trust when it ends and is distributed. A successor trustee is a person whom you, the creator of the trust, place in charge when you die or become incapacitated if you are the trustee of the living trust. Sometimes, there is a need for a designated person to manage the beneficiaries if there are children who are minors listed as beneficiaries.

The trustee or successor trustee is someone whom you should trust and whom you know has your best intentions at heart. Most people will select their spouse, their child, or a close, trusted family member or friend to handle this job.

The process of establishing a living trust is not necessarily difficult in concept, but it does require the help of a skilled attorney. The hardest parts to creating a trust are simple legal jargon issues. For example, working with an estate planning attorney will help you to define what the property in the trust is and who will be in each role in the trust, and will help you determine how the trust is amended and how much power the trustee is given, in addition to other details.

Why a living trust?

There is more to learn about trusts, discussed in Chapter 7. But do not write off living trusts just yet; there are many benefits to using them. This is one of the most used documents by those who want to have something else in place over a will. The following are some of the benefits that you will gain from a living trust.

If you have real property, such as real estate and investment properties, you do not want to allow these properties to go through probate, as that would decrease their value substantially. A living trust may be the answer.

Make sure to talk with your tax advisor on the effects that a trust will have on your taxes. Currently, Virginia does not have an inheritance tax and tracks the federal exemption for estate tax. Federal estate taxes are in flux, though, which means state taxes may be up for change as well. Keep abreast of the possible changes that may be happening in this regard.

But by far, there are many other advantages to a living trust that should be considered. For example, the main reason for them is the fact that you can better control what happens to your estate. You have the ability to better plan for your estate and to protect it from probate; you have the ability to predict what happens in the future with better accuracy, and you have the ability to make changes. You can name additional, alternative beneficiaries, and you can name someone to keep your children's interests at heart if you die while they are minors.

If you and your spouse own property together through a living trust and are both named co-trustees and co-trustors, the other gains ownership of the property when one dies. There is no need for it to go through probate. And when the survivor also dies, the house passes through the living trust to whomever was designated to get it, again avoiding the probate process. If you did not have this in place, the property could have been subjected to the fees of the probate process twice.

By setting up and managing your trust now, you also allow yourself to see what will happen to your estate when you are gone. For example, if you set up your trust to provide for your heirs to manage your investments and they do not do well with it or become untrustworthy, you can make changes to your trust while you are still alive and therefore protect your estate from failure. You can do this with numerous aspects, such as donations and other distributions that you set up. If you do not like how they are being handled, you can make changes so that your funds are not being wasted, or perhaps you would like to give them more for a job well-done.

While there are benefits to living trusts, working with your estate planning attorney and tax advisor is critical to setting one up correctly.

The pitfalls of a living trust

Like everything else in estate planning, there has to be a downside to a living trust. While these disadvantages are important to note, you should consider how they affect you individually.

One of the greatest problems with a living trust stems from the fact that you have to fund a living trust while you are living, which means that the funds and property need to transfer hands when the trust is put into action. Each time that you desire to have your trust property change hands — you gain or lose an investment or transfer real estate, for example — the trust has to be updated again. This can pose a real problem, or rather hassle, to those who are investors and make changes regularly.

Another problem arises when you do not put property into the living trust. For example, let us say that you get an inheritance from your Aunt Sue, but you forget to put it into your trust officially. If you do not do this, those funds are considered to be probate-required assets because they never were part of the trust. Therefore, they will go through the probate process.

If this happens, the Virginia courts could be faced with determining what you intended. Did you intend the trust to be funded, even though you did not do it formally? Does the trust therefore supersede the assets that are part of the probate estate? If there are insufficient assets to fund the purpose designed and stated in your trust, this could be a moot point, but suppose there are ample estate assets that could satisfy all or a substantial portion of the trust you created. Further, suppose the fiduciary of your probate estate or your heirs to the probate estate are not happy about the provisions of the trust, or the beneficiaries of the trust make a claim on the estate for the funds. You can readily see the battle that will engage.

A word of warning for you about planners who are trying to sell you on the idea of a living trust: If you are considering purchasing and setting one up because you have been sold the idea, make sure you use a trusted financial planner and estate planning attorney. Do not go with the ad you saw in the paper, as you want to make sure that the costs are not being inflated for their benefit.

There are good and bad aspects of a living trust. If you want to play an active role in what will happen to your estate when you are gone, then a living trust can be a good option for you. If you want to find success in putting a will together and forgetting about it, a living trust may not be for you. With careful planning and execution, though, living trusts can be a good solution for substituting a will. Work with your attorney to determine the right solution for your situation.

Joint Tenancy Bank Accounts

Another option that you have for funding your estate needs is that of a joint tenancy bank account. If you are considering this type of account, you will find some good benefits from it. Like joint tenancy, this form offers the same type of joint holding of the account. Both (or multiple) individuals are in charge of the account, hold equal ownership of it, and can get out of it any time they want to. To get out of it, they simply withdraw the funds that are in the bank account. A bank account serves as the property in this case.

As with a joint tenancy, the person that survives the other will then take ownership of the entire account. There is no need for probate with this type of account. And if the bank accounts are under multiple people's names, they each get an equal share of the deceased person's equal percentage.

Tenancy by the Entirety

Tenancy by the entirety is another solution for will substitutes, recognized in Virginia as noted above.

For states that permit it, the mechanism is like that of joint tenancy with one real difference — only spouses can use it. Therefore, you can only have two people holding the joint tenancy.

In tenancy by the entirety, the rights of survivorship are in play, which means that when one spouse dies, the other will gain ownership of the rest of the property. This also means that there is no need to pass through probate because the tenancy overrules any will or state laws that are in place. The property automatically transfers from the deceased spouse's possession to that of the surviving spouse. Another difference is that with tenancy by the entirety, there is no ability to transfer your funds to someone else should you wish to. The only way that this could happen would be through consent or notification of the other spouse.

Payable-on-Death Accounts

For those who are considering a simpler method of will substitution, that could be the payable-on-death (POD) accounts. These are not as well-known as a living trust or a joint tenancy, but are still good considerations if your situation fits. These types of accounts are just what they sound like: When you set up the account, you simply list whom you wish to be your beneficiary on the account.

There are several types of these that can be used for bank accounts, car registration, and real estate. Each of these payable-on-death accounts allows you to name someone to claim them when you die. In most cases, the individual simply needs to bring in a copy of your death certificate and some personal identification for themselves. They take this information to the title holder or holder of the account and then are able to transfer the property into their name, claiming full ownership of it. Again, there is no need to pass through probate and be taxed as such.

The one important aspect of POD accounts that you must realize is that these accounts often require some monitoring. For example, if you have set up a POD account for each of your three grandchildren, you should go back and take a closer look at those accounts every so often because they may earn interest or otherwise increase in value at different rates, and therefore, the ending balance may not be what you want it to be. If each child is supposed to receive an equal amount, but one account does not perform well, this could be a problem.

Yet the benefit of POD accounts is the fact that they are so easy to manage. You can make changes to them at any time, and make any changes that you would like to, for as long as you live. Therefore, you can go in and change the amounts, change whom you wish to give the funds to by listing a new beneficiary, and even use the funds if you need and want to. These are some of the most flexible options available because of how fast they transfer and how easy they are to manage.

Other Will Substitutes

There are a handful of other will substitutes that are available for your use. Each of these can be useful, even though some may seem simple to use and may not even seem like will substitutes. But using these substitutes is a way to sidestep probate and still get the funds and property that you own to your beneficiary as quickly as possible.

Savings bonds

One option is a savings bond — yes, the same old bonds that you likely used to consider purchasing. It is not uncommon for people to purchase them and stash them away for a rainy day — or to leave for their beneficiaries — and accumulate thousands of them. This is a good way to transfer your funds to someone else upon your death, but it is also a way for you to accumulate some interest on the funds that you are socking away. Since bonds double in value over time and are one of the safest types of investments, they are ideal for most individuals to use for their beneficiaries.

There are two types of savings bonds, each with their own benefits. One is called an alternative payee option, which is a savings bond that works much like a joint tenancy. Both of you are listed on the savings bond, and both of you can cash them in at any time. But when one dies, the other has the full ownership of the bond. This happens through the rights to survivorship.

The other type of savings bond is called a beneficiary payee. In this type of savings bond, there is a beneficiary listed on the bond. When you — the bond owner — die, the savings bond transfers to the person that you have listed as a beneficiary. In this case, the bond transfers the same basic way that other property would transfer through a will.

You may need to talk to your financial planner and tax advisor about savings bonds. There may be a need for taxes on these bonds, depending on the way that you have them set up. In addition, you should include them as a positive tool in your estate planning.

Retirement accounts

If you have retirement accounts, you may already have a will substitution in place. Those who are using 401(k)s or even IRAs have a built-in plan already in the works. In most of these types of accounts, the individual who is adding to the account is able to list their beneficiaries, or the people who are going to get a share of their funds when they die.

For example, if you have a 401(k) set up, as part of that process, you will list a beneficiary who will take claim over your account when you die. This allows you to easily provide funds for that person upon your death. Setting up a 401(k) or other retirement account is relatively simple, especially when your employer is sponsoring one.

An aspect that you should especially take note of about these retirement accounts is the tax implications of them. Depending on the type of account that you have and how and where it is set up, your beneficiaries may need to pay taxes on the funds that they receive. Talk to your tax advisor about the best route to take with these. Also, your financial planner can help you choose the right one for you. There are various retirement-oriented investment options out there today that can be quite beneficial, no matter where you are in the estate planning process.

Deeds

Deeds are titles to real estate, such as your house and other real property that you own. A deed, though, is a useful tool in estate planning. A deed can be used to move your property from your possession to that of your beneficiary when you die.

There are some tricky aspects to doing this, though. If it is shown that your deed was changed to reflect a property transfer at the grantor's death, this could be shown as a possible problem, and therefore, the deed could be rejected.

With deeds, you will want to work closely with your attorney. There is specific wording that must be included in the deed to make sure that it provides for what you wish it to. You can use these to help you put your house into the hands of your son or daughter, for example, with language written into the deed. Because a deed is legal evidence that real estate ownership is held by someone, it has the power of being a will substitution that is direct and straightforward when written correctly.

If you wish to use deeds as your means of transferring property, work closely with your estate planner to make this happen. You can do it yourself, but it is a safe bet to work with an attorney who can make sure your wishes are carried out legally.

Summing It Up

Now that we have plowed through all the various ways that you can avoid probate, it is still important for you to realize that any of these mechanisms should be backed up with a basic will. As you will see later on, developing an estate that encompasses all your wishes is a process of finding the right tool to make your wish come true. When you have an idea of what options are out there, you can make a good decision about what to do to make that happen.

Although most of these elements could be done by you alone, it pays to work with your estate planning team. They will ensure that you take the right route for your particular situation.

CASE STUDY: TAXES AND GIFTS: THE MYSTERIES

David J. Bernstein, Attorney at Law
33111 Seneca Drive
Solon, Ohio 44139
(440) 349-4889
Web site: **www.estatefacts.com**

The tax laws are not designed to protect your estate. Instead, they are designed to take away from your estate as much as possible in order to raise revenue for the federal and state governments. The estate laws of each state do provide some protection to you, but they are designed to put the rights of your creditors first and your beneficiaries last. A competent estate planning attorney can design your estate plan to minimize taxes and preserve as much of your estate as possible.

As technology has advanced, the process for estate planning has become easier and simpler. Estate planning professionals typically have your estate plan fully in place in just a few days or weeks. The client's time can be minimized to just a few hours.

One of the big mistakes that I see in estate plans is to leave a single dollar to someone whom you do not want to leave anything. This is not the right way to do this. It may cost thousands of dollars for the administrator to hire an investigator to track down an estranged heir to deliver the single dollar. The best language is to name the person being left out and state that they are intentionally omitted. Stating the reason could lead to a successful challenge if it is not worded properly, so it is better not to state the reason. Disinherited persons may wish to contest not being included, but they must prove that you were incompetent or unaware of your family, your environment, or your estate, or that there was fraud, mistake, or undue influence at the time you signed the estate plan. Without one or more of these elements, they have no hope of winning.

For gifts, the right choice to go with is dependent on what the client wants to see happen. I tell my clients that they do not know how much money they will need to live on for the rest of their lives. If they start giving it away before they die, it may not be available in a time of need. Gifting is typically only best for the very wealthy who know that their financial needs will be met no matter what happens.

There is plenty of hope if planning takes place before your incapacity. You can handpick who will take over, without the interference of any outsider. If no plan is in place at the time of your incapacity, you may find yourself at the discretion of the probate court and a court-appointed guardian (who may also be a probate attorney), which could cost your estate tens of thousands of dollars per year.

James River Bridge, Newport, Virginia

Chapter 7

Trusts: Trusting and Your Estate

There is so much to be gained when the right person uses a trust in the right manner for their estate planning goals. If you are considering a trust, though, you should ensure you are working closely with your tax advisor, financial planner, and your estate planning attorney to make it as tight as possible so that your goals are met throughout the process.

A living trust is like a will with one huge benefit: You can use it instead of a will and avoid probate. One important thing to know is that until you die, the property in the trust is still essentially yours to do with what you will. Of course, should you make changes, you should go back and alter the documentation in the trust to match your requirements and desires. Yet there are many different ways to use a trust besides just the living trust that we have described.

For example, if you have a disabled child, you may be worried about their care after you are gone. You can set up a trust for that child that does not just pay out when you die, but continues to care for the child as you have seen fit for years after you are gone. You can also use these trusts to control property that is left to someone else and to provide for your children from a previous marriage.

A living trust is not the right choice for everyone. Most people can use and benefit from them, but not everyone needs to use them. For example, if you are young and healthy, the cost of setting up and managing a trust now may be too much for something that you may not really need later. In this case, a will can cover the important facts if you should die suddenly. In addition, those who are going through divorce and those who have little property will not find much use for a trust.

Another time when trusts are not necessarily the best tool is when any of the other will substitution devices we have mentioned may work better for you. In addition, those who have debt problems, especially those who are in high amounts of debt or those who are facing legal issues, may want to go through probate to have their creditors limited in what they can claim. Of course, if you do not have anyone whom you can trust to manage the trust after you are gone, that too is a reason not to use this type of will avoidance tool.

Work with your attorney to determine whether a trust is the right thing for your situation.

How Trusts Work

You can set up a trust to maintain complete control of your funds in your trust for as long as you are alive. That means that you can have the benefit of moving property and making decisions that are based on what is happening now in your life. And more importantly, once you are gone, the trust can no longer be changed. What you have left there, how you have divided it and how you have decided it would be used is the way it has to be. Your successor trustee can then immediately hand over the property to the people named as your beneficiaries, and within a matter of weeks, they could have their property, though they must first go through legally changing ownership of the items through documentation.

Trusts and taxes

You may still get the same benefits in tax savings on your home when it is included in a trust. For example, if you own a home with a mortgage and place the home into a trust for your child when you die, you still get to reap the benefits of deducting mortgage interest from your income tax form. If you decide to sell your home, you can do so every two years and then exclude some $250,000 of capital gains — or up to $500,000 for a couple — from taxes, too. This is the same thing as having property that is not included in your trust.

You must also take into consideration the estate tax. Do not make the mistake of believing that an estate tax does not have to be paid if you have a trust in place. It quite possibly will still need to be paid, even though you are avoiding probate. But you can work with your estate planning attorney to work out a better arrangement that can help you avoid some of those costly taxes — for example, if you set up a trust that will avoid probate and then in that trust establish another trust that will pay out funds to children or spouses, helping you avoid some of the estate taxes. This is called an AB trust, also known as a credit shelter trust. AB trusts are discussed further in Chapter 9. They are often used in Virginia and other states where circumstances warrant, such as wealthy estates that are likely to exceed the federal estate tax exclusion. When Congress legislated no estate tax for 2010, it appeared that AB trusts might have lost their allure, but that is only a one-year window. With the reinstatement of $1 million as the threshold in 2011, and additional changes in the law in question, AB trusts are holding their own. Consult with your estate planning team about whether an AB trust makes sense for your financial circumstances.

Trusts for Couples

You do not have to be single to use a living trust effectively. It is still one of the best tools to use when it comes to will avoidance for couples. Or, if it offers better advantages for you, each of the individuals in a marriage can have an individual trust established, with benefits from them. This works the best when there is property that is divided between the two, as opposed to having mostly shared property. As with most trusts, given the variations possible, this is an option that should be discussed with an estate planning attorney.

If you have shared property, you do not want to go with an individual trust because that would mean dividing up any shared property between the two of you. On the other hand, if you have shared property and individual property as well, you can include both in the trust. In this example, you can have separate beneficiaries listed for your share of the property.

When you have this type of trust established, when the first spouse dies, their share of the trust property is split apart and given to whomever he or she lists as their beneficiaries. Most of the time, this is going to be the surviving spouse or children, but whomever he or she has listed as their beneficiaries will get their share of the trust.

Creating the Trust

Now that you have some more information about trusts, it is time to determine whether you should use one. Let us break down the questions that you have to ask to determine whether it is the right tool for you. You have to determine what you will put into the trust and whom you will name as your successor trustee, whom you will name as your beneficiaries, and how debts will be paid once the trust is put into place.

What property?

First and foremost, what property will you include in your trust? Most people want to include as much valuable property in their trust as possible and therefore keep it from going through probate. Unless you have some other way of avoiding probate for your more valuable property, it should be put into a trust. If you establish another means of doing this, the property does not need to enter into the trust as well.

You can use a trust for some of your property and allow other will substitutions to work for the rest. For example, you may have already established a pay-upon-death bank account for your son, and therefore, this does not need to enter into the trust.

If you put real estate into your trust, there is the benefit of possibly avoiding reappraisal of your property, such as is usually required in the probate process. For example, if you live in a state that requires an appraisal be done if a new owner is placed on the title (not usually required in Virginia), this could be costly if you were to move from your current situation into, say, a joint tenancy agreement. But if you instead include it in your trust, there is no need for this change to happen. That is because the government does not recognize the trust as being separate from you until you have died.

Also important to note is your standing with your mortgage. Sometimes individuals worry about what happens to their mortgage when they place their property into a living trust. Do not worry; because the federal government does not recognize the trust while you are alive, you do not have to do anything with your mortgage when you place your home into your trust.

DO NOT NOTIFY MORTGAGE CO OR INSURANCE CO. – to avoid unnecessary hassles

You do not need to notify your mortgage company. Federal law also prohibits the transferring of your home into a trust from being a reason to "call" the mortgage due. Your insurance company also does not need to be notified. If you do notify them, you may have an increase in your rates. Telling your mortgage company or insurance company just creates hassles for you; do not bother with the struggle.

Who will be your trustees?

Having determined the property you want to place in your trust, you need to now name your trustees.

- Whom will you name as the initial trustee?
- Whom will you name as the successor trustee?

As for the initial trustee, this is likely to be you. If you and your spouse will enter into the trust together, you can both serve as co-trustees, having equal shares of ownership in the trust. Being the trustee of your trust is important because it provides you with the power to manage your trust until you die.

Technically, you can name someone else as the initial trustee, but that may not be the best route for most individuals. You will have to go into a complicated process that often has legal implications. In addition, you will need separate trust records, and a trust tax return will need to be filed with the Internal Revenue Service (IRS). This process is costly and long, but if you want to do it, talk to your estate planning attorney about it first.

You can also name several people as co-trustees of the property. If you cannot or do not want to manage your property while you are alive, you can set up the trust so that you and others are listed as co-trustees, which helps to circumvent the IRS and still allows you to pass control of your property to someone else.

Next, you need to pick your successor trustee. Your successor trustee takes over for you once you have died. If you are a co-trustee with your spouse, your successor trustee will take over when both of the trustees have died. The successor trustee is responsible for managing and distributing your trust to your beneficiaries after you are gone. You should also include an alternative successor trustee. If your successor trustee should no longer be able to serve as your trustee after you have died, or even dies before you, the alternative will take over.

The successor trustee has a simple job, especially when everything has been clearly defined for him, but there is a bit more to the process than just what has been included here. He or she will be responsible for getting several copies of your death certificate and will need to have copies of the living trust. He or she will have to provide documentation of the trust, his or her identity, and the death certificates to make claims on the property and funds as described in the trust. Do not worry, though; financial institutions deal with successor trustees all the time, and there is no real problem for those that have to do this.

Another responsibility that successor trustees have to take on is that of preparing documents that need to have title transfers or other such elements. For example, they will need to help prepare documents for real estate transfers, which will include helping to get the title transferred, signing for it, and also recording the transfer with your county's public records office.

Of course, the successor trustee also must make sure that home furnishings and mementos are distributed as you have declared in your trust. If you decided that your $100,000 painting collection should go to your third cousin, then your successor trustee must make sure that those paintings end up in your third cousin's hands.

Your trustee will need to notify your beneficiaries of your death and that the trust has become irrevocable — which means it can no longer be changed because you have died. Your estate planning attorney will be able to help you make this happen. Notification that the trust is irrevocable, who the successor trustee is, the date that the trust went into effect, and a statement that allows the beneficiary to receive a copy of the trust should be provided to all beneficiaries listed in the trust. Doing this keeps the successor trustee out of lawsuits.

Who are your beneficiaries?

Your beneficiaries are those who will receive your property through the trust. You can name your spouse, your children, or anyone whom you would like to in your trust to receive all or part of your property. Your beneficiaries will be listed for only your half of the trust, and your co-trustee will be able to list their beneficiaries, too, if you have formed a trust as a couple. The beneficiaries do not have to be the same.

While you do not have to tell your beneficiaries that you are including them in your trust and what they will get, this often makes the job of the successor trustee much easier. As we have talked about, it is important to keep an open dialogue between you and your beneficiaries so that they know exactly who will get what. This helps to dissipate problems and hurt feelings later. With a trust, you can make any changes that you find are necessary throughout your lifetime.

Work with your attorney to determine whether there is any need to create an AB trust (discussed further in Chapter 9), or other types of trusts that may have additional benefits for tax breaks. In addition, you may have special-needs cases, such as property that needs to be managed for minor children until they are old enough. When included in your trust, special language is needed to ensure that your beneficiaries receive what they should get, but with special consideration of their and your needs.

Naming your beneficiaries is one of the toughest jobs you have, but it is a process that can be changed and tweaked over time with a revocable trust.

How will debt be handled?

If you place most or all your debt in a living trust, there may be a problem with paying off any debts that you have. Like most people, you may have promised yourself that there is no need to worry about debt because you plan to have everything paid in full when you die. However, good intentions do not always play out. If you end up in the hospital with costly medical bills, how will they be paid? If you die suddenly, and your house is still mortgaged, how will this be paid? Handling debt questions now while setting up your living trust is important.

In most cases, a mortgage is not a problem because the mortgage will pass on to whomever you have left the house. In standard practice, your successor trustee will pay off all the debts that you have using the property in the trust before it is given out to anyone. But it is wiser to have a specific amount set aside in the trust to make these types of payments so that everyone gets what they were supposed to.

You should also monitor your living trust while alive and the value of it in relation to your debt. In estate planning, you want to figure in the debt as part of your estate plan so that no one else has to pay it out of their share of your estate. These types of considerations indicate how important it is to get advice from an expert.

Making Your Trust Valid

One of the most important areas for you to consider is whether the trust is valid. In the wording and the structure of the trust, you will need to set up and maintain this aspect. Again, working with your attorney is a must, if only for this reason alone. You should understand how a trust is set up so that it is valid and will do what you wish it to do.

Step 1: Preparing the documents

First, do not be fooled into thinking that there is a "one way is the only way" philosophy when it comes to creating a living trust document. The fact is, there is no legal form that must be used. Working with your attorney, you can create a simple form that will include what the document is and that defines all the terms of the trust. All the important individuals whom we have talked about, from the trustor and the successor trustee down to the beneficiaries, need to be spelled out. You need to identify all your property in the trust and where it will go (and how) to your beneficiaries. Although no witnesses are required, you should have it notarized, which means signing the trust in front of a notary. It is imperative that you do have it notarized, rather than using bank guarantees or other options, as it is only official once it has been notarized.

Step 2: Transferring to the trustee

Next, you need to transfer the trust property into the trustee's name. If you do not make this formal step, the successor trustee will not be able to perform his or her duties to the fullest. What this means is simply assigning your name to all documents in a specific format. It should read, "John Doe, as trustee for John Doe Trust" on the documents.

The property that will be placed into your trust that has a title or otherwise has legal paperwork that shows its ownership is the first type of property to make this change with. This includes your real estate; bank accounts; vehicles; safe deposit boxes; stocks and bonds; partnerships, including corporations and limited partnerships; mutual funds; and money market accounts. All these have a title or ownership papers that need to be transferred into the trustee's name as we have described.

Some property does not have any such documentation for ownership. Your jewelry, household items, clothing, cash, and any other type of valuable property that you will be placing into your trust without documentation for ownership still need some additional attention. To transfer these items into the trustee's name, you will simply include them in a list format on your paperwork with a "Notice of Assignment" listed with them, which transfers ownership.

Step 3: Maintaining your trust over time

Just setting up your trust is not enough to keep it going. The trust is unique from most other forms of wills and substitutions because at any time, it can be revoked or otherwise changed to fit what is happening now in your life. Therefore, it does take some effort to maintain your trust. But that is not necessarily a negative thing.

If you acquire additional property that you want placed into your trust, make this necessary change. If you sell off property or want to remove it from your trust, this needs to be changed as well. You may also want to revisit your trust often to make sure that the amount that you have left to your beneficiaries is accurate. For example, one account can suddenly increase in value moreso than the other, and if you wanted them to be equal, you may need to make some changes to the trust to show this. In addition, lifestyle changes such as the addition of children, divorce, or marriage need to be updated as soon as possible.

If you have a shared trust, though, this will need to be updated not just by you, but also by your co-trustee or spouse.

Some important notes to consider in regard to maintaining your trust include the following:

- **Amending your trust is a right that you have until your death.** You can amend the documents by having amendments added to the document that have been signed by you and witnessed by a notary. Amendments work well for making small or simple changes, such as adding your beneficiary to the document or moving one piece of property to the trust. But when large changes need to be made, revoking the old trust and installing a new one is easier.

- **You can add additional property to your trust.** When you do this, you should be transferring it into the trustee's name, adding it to your living trust documentation with signature and notary, and naming the beneficiary. You may need to make changes to what you already have in your trust if you deem it necessary in allocating assets to your beneficiaries.

- **Your trust property can be sold or even refinanced during the time that you own it.** You can do so by selling it right out of the trust, or you can transfer it back into your sole name from the trust name, and then sell it. You may need to work with a title company for real estate transfers to ensure that the correct method is used. You should then amend your living trust documents to show the changes that you have made.

- **You also can completely revoke the trust.** If you decide to do this, you will simply provide a signed and notarized document that says so. Sometimes you do need both spouses to sign for this, but more often, only one has to make this change.

Abstract of Trust

Suppose you do not want everyone to know what your trust will include until after your death. An abstract of trust is a type of trust that can be used to accomplish this. This tool allows you to say that your trust exists and that it is going to be used, but it simply is a "short list" of what is included in that trust, rather than spelling it all out.

You may want to do this if a financial institution wants to have documentation that a trust exists, but you do not want to provide them with any details, which legally you do not have to do. Therefore, an abstract of trust is formed. In some states, this document is a specific form that must be completed, whereas in other states, it is not. In Virginia, there is not a statutory form, but banks and title companies (where real estate is involved) may have their own forms. When you work with your estate planning attorney, you will be better able to make sure that the right forms and documentation are provided to draw up this type of trust.

Summing It Up

Now that you have had the opportunity to explore the world of a living trust, you may be ready to dive right in. Before you do that, make sure that you work with your team of advisors in making the decisions that will affect your trust as well as the rest of your estate plan. For many people, the wisest decision is to create a living trust as part of the estate plan, but not as the only part of that estate plan. Finding the right solution for you will take a few more minutes. In the next chapters, we will help you to develop a total estate plan that encompasses everything that you need and want to include.

State Capitol Building, Richmond, Virginia

Chapter 8

Taxes: Estate Tax and Other Taxes

One of the largest, most complex areas of estate planning is the tax involved with it. Estate tax is an important part of planning your estate because it will take a large chunk of money from what you leave to your heirs. There are several types of taxes that could affect your estate, depending on your circumstances. These include:

- Federal estate tax
- State estate tax
- Inheritance tax
- Gift tax

As part of the planning for your estate, you need to take into consideration each of these types and make changes or allotments to your estate to accommodate them if they apply.

Anyone who is living in the United States or is a U.S. citizen is required to pay federal estate taxes. All your property in the United States is taxable. Yet there are some strange laws in place to determine how much you need to pay. In the last several years, Congress has passed new laws that define this information. As of publication, here is what you need to know:

- For a death that occurred in 2007 or 2008, a personal exemption of $2 million applied at the highest death estate tax rate of 45 percent.
- In 2009, the amount of personal exemption rises to $3.5 million at 45 percent.
- In 2010, there is no estate tax, as it is repealed.
- In 2011, it comes back with an amount of personal exemption at $1 million, unless the repeal is changed by Congress before this time. The estate tax rate is 55 percent in 2011.
- At the time of publication, President Barack Obama and Congress plan to revisit the repeal of the estate tax before the end of 2009. If the Government decided to suspend the repeal, or enact other changes, these stipulations could change.

The state of the law is thus uncertain. There are political as well as economic reasons for the use of this tax, and therefore, there is no way to know which way it will go.

Most estate planners and tax professionals will tell you to plan your estate the best that you can through 2013 for federal estate taxes. As changes in the law occur, you will need to revisit your estate planning.

The point is to understand and plan for these taxes. Let us take a closer look at some of points you need to fully understand.

Federal Estate Tax Exemptions

For many people, there is no need to worry about this tax because the value of their estate is not large enough to be affected. There are several exemptions that you can take into consideration for your estate plan. Here is a breakdown of them.

Personal exemption

Depending on the year of death and the whim of Congress, as noted above, the personal exemption will apply from $1 to $3.5 million. One important note is that if you leave gifts that are taxable during your lifetime, this reduces your exemption amount.

Marital deduction

Another deduction for which you may qualify is the marital deduction. This means that all property you leave to your spouse, if he or she is a U.S. citizen, is exempt from taxes. If not a U.S. citizen, this deduction does not apply. So far, this deduction does not change year to year, as in the personal exemption. You must be legally married for this exemption to be used. Terms like "significant other" or "mates" are not recognized by this deduction.

Yet there is a potential problem with this. If you die and leave all your property to your spouse, he or she now has more personal property, which could aggregate the estate to exceed the allowable personal exemption (called the estate tax threshold). The best way around this is to take steps to plan your estate with this in mind, making sure that both spouses can benefit from it.

You can avoid this tax trap by planning an AB trust — discussed later in Chapter 9 — for your needs. In this case, the spouses place all or most of their property into the trust. When one spouse dies, the surviving spouse still has access to the trust property and can use it as needed, but does not own the property outright, which means it is not subject to the tax.

If you are married to a non-citizen, it is important for you to consider the best route to take in leaving property to your spouse. There are several ways around the rule that you cannot leave them property without tax implications. First, if the property is under the exemption threshold, the tax burden will not apply. You can also create a qualified domestic trust. These trusts are complex, and the use of an estate planning attorney is critical.

Charitable deductions

For those who are rather wealthy, it may be best to use charitable deductions. Gifts to charities are tax-exempt, assuming you give them to a recognized tax-exempt charity. For this purpose, you will want to work with an attorney to help you set up a charitable remainder trust. Before you die, you will need to make a gift to a charity in trust. Then, you can receive a certain annual income from the gift property while you are alive. You will need to pay income tax on this throughout your lifetime.

State Estate Tax and Inheritance Tax

The state takes another look at your tax situation and then assesses their claim to your property when you die. There are two types of taxes to consider here: state estate tax and inheritance tax.

Inheritance tax

Only certain states levy this tax. As of May 2009, they are:

- Nebraska
- New Jersey
- Kentucky

- Oregon
- Pennsylvania
- Tennessee
- Maryland
- Iowa
- Indiana

This tax is for all property that is left by a state resident, no matter where that property is located, and all real estate within the state — no matter where the property owner died — is taxable.

In order for you to learn what these taxes are, you do need to invest in a bit of research or the help of your estate planning team. Each state has a bit of a different situation and varying rules that must be followed. Indeed, there are ways to work around the amount of taxes you need to pay, with assistance of legal counsel.

State estate tax

Because of the decrease in the federal estate tax laws, many states have now implemented new laws in the form of state estate taxes. Before 2005, states used to have a "pick up" tax, which is a tax that they received as part of the federal estate taxes that were assessed to the estate. But, under these new laws, this is no more. Because the need for these funds is still there, many states have created their own state estate tax. Currently Virginia follows the federal program, but stay tuned for possible changes in the future.

Gift Tax

In an effort to prevent people from giving away all their property before they die and avoiding any estate tax by doing so, Congress developed the gift tax. Gift tax rates are the same as estate tax rates. What is more, this tax is applied not to the recipient of the gift, but to the person who is giving the gift.

As we mentioned, the estate tax is in the process of being repealed and starts again in 2011. While your estate tax exemption rate will change as determined by those laws (see the preceding section on federal estate tax), the gift tax exemption stays at $1 million. This means that those who die before 2010 will be able to leave more property without giving it as a gift at the tax-free rate. However, these stipulations could change should Congress and President Obama revisit the repeal of the tax.

Another important part of this tax is to understand when it affects you. If you make a gift that is taxable, you do not pay the tax on it at that time; rather, your estate will pay the tax when it is deducted from your estate tax exemption after your death.

There are also several exemptions available for gift taxes. These can help you lower the amount of tax you end up paying.

Annual exemption

IRS estate and gift tax laws provide you with an exemption amount on a per year basis. For example, this is currently $13,000. You can give away $13,000 per year tax-free, and this does not change with the next estate tax laws. If you are married, both spouses can give separate $13,000 gifts.

This is a "per recipient" law. For example, you can give $13,000 to your daughter and another $13,000 to your son. There is also the notion of gift splitting, where you will be apportioning the value the gift that is given. For example, if you and your spouse give a gift of $16,000 to your sister and give another $18,000 to your brother-in-law, you would have gone over the $13,000 gift limit per person if it was given singly. But because you split this (or you each gave half), it is considered that you each gave your sister $8,000 and your brother-in-law $9,000. Neither of these is over the limit.

If you are younger, you can give away a considerable amount of your money and property this way. You should also take note that, as the cost of living rises, this gift tax exemption is likely to rise as well. But the cost of living must have a cumulative raise in the current exemption by more than $1,000 before it will rise to $14,000.

Marital exemption

Any gift that you give to your spouse is tax-exempt no matter how much it is. As part of the marital exemption for federal estate tax, this law is in effect. Again, if you are not legally married or are not married to a U.S. citizen, this is not allowable. For those who are married to someone who is a non-citizen, you can give up to $117,000 per year to them without any taxes. By giving your non-citizen spouse this sum over the course of time, you can effectively leave them with a tax-free estate.

Medical bills and school tuition

Another exemption that may apply is when you pay someone else's medical bills or their school tuition. To use this type of exemption, though, you must pay the provider of the service directly. If you give the funds to your son for example, who is a student, it no longer is tax-free (unless the gift tax exemption applies), even if he uses it to pay his tuition. In addition, if the student already paid for his education, you cannot reimburse him for the funds for tax savings. Things like room and board do not qualify, either — just the cost of tuition.

GSTT — Generation Skipping Transfer Tax

Another type of tax to be considered is the Generation Skipping Transfer Tax (GSTT). This tax came to be due to the number of people who were skipping their children and leaving their property to their grandchildren. In doing so, they avoided taxing their property two times — once when passed down from grandparent to child and then second from child to grandchild. This new tax is a large one and effectively stops most people from avoiding taxes in this manner.

If you do want to leave funds in this manner, work closely with your estate planning attorney, who may be able to assist in lowering the GSTT amount that you have to pay. This is a complex method of estate planning and one that is best left to the specialist. For those who have a sizable estate, this could be an important consideration.

Estate Recovery Act

Although the Estate Recovery Act is not a tax, it is important to mention here, as it involves your estate's funds. If you have used Medicaid benefits throughout your life, you need to consider how it will affect your estate when you are gone. In 1993, Congress passed the Estate Recovery Act; this act provides for repayment of Medicaid benefits for certain individuals. That means that if you drew on these funds, you may have to pay them back.

The hardest part of this act is that most people who have to use Medicaid have less property or fewer assets. For many, the only value comes through with the home that they own.

Some states have a homestead exemption or personal residence waiver that you can use as an exemption to this act. Each state has a different type of exemption here, if they have one. Virginia does.

Virginia Code section 34-4 provides that "every householder" may "hold exempt from creditor process arising out of a debt, real and personal property, or either, to be selected by the householder, including money and debts due the householder not exceeding $5,000 in value." In addition, each householder is entitled to an additional $500 exemption per each dependant.

These exemptions can mean the difference between losing the family's home or not. If you draw on Medicaid for any reason, find out whether it might have to be repaid after your death. If so, work with your estate planning team to protect your assets from this repayment if possible.

How is Inherited Property Valued?

Let us look at how your property is valued to determine where it stands as far as estate tax goes.

The tax basis is the value that is assigned to the property from which taxable gain or loss on a sale is determined. This means that when property is purchased, its basis tends to be the cost. For example, let us say that you purchase something valued at $10,000, and then sell it for $21,000. The sale price ($21,000) minus the basis ($10,000) equals the taxable gain on the asset (in this case, $11,000). In accordance with this, the original cost basis will be adjusted up, such as for improvements, or down, for depreciation. If you made improvements to your home that increased its value, the improvement value is added to the basis of the property. In loose terms, capital improvement is anything that lasts for over one year.

Now, when you take this into consideration with estate tax, note that federal tax laws say that the basis of inherited property is raised to the fair market value of the property at the time of the deceased owner's death. Up or down, it is determined by what the fair market value of the property is.

When more than one person owns the property (joint tenancy property), only the portion of the property that is owned by the person who dies is raised or lowered to fair market value. The others will continue to have the same basis of value that they had originally.

For estate planning, this means that in almost all cases, it is more desirable to hold on to appreciated property until after you die and allow it to pass through ownership after death. This way, those who inherit the property will have the benefit of the raised value of the property. If it is sold prior to this, there would be capital gains taxes that would need to be paid, plus income taxes to the state. But if your property is sold after your death, there is no tax assessed on it.

You cannot use this formula for calculating gifts that are made during your lifetime. Only property that changes hands after death will qualify for it.

Now that you understand a bit more about what taxes are out there, it is time to take a closer look at how you can reduce what has to be paid.

Chapter 9

Lowering Your Federal Estate Taxes

It would be nice if you did not have to pay any federal estate taxes (or any taxes, for that matter). But the next best thing to do is to consider how you can reduce what you have to pay in federal estate taxes.

It is important to do all that you can — within legal restraints — to avoid paying high tax rates. In most cases, you will not be able to avoid all your taxes, or even most of them. For those who are quite wealthy, there are always strings and loopholes to be found, but an expert attorney will be necessary for this — even good financial planning attorneys will point you down the clear path rather than one filled with risky maneuvers.

There are two ways in which anyone can reduce the estate tax they pay:

1. Make gifts during your lifetime.
2. Use an irrevocable trust.

Making Gifts During Your Life

One of the first and best ways to lower what you have to pay is to have less to pay on. If you give away your property while you are still alive, you will remove any potential tax on that estate after your death — you no longer own it, after all. There are several factors to consider here. Let us break them down.

Federal gift tax exclusion

You can make gifts of up to $13,000 per person per calendar year that are considered tax-free. When you use this method to reduce your taxes, you will remove a substantial amount over the course of time (you can give away more than $13,000 per year, if you give it to several people). If you have children, grandchildren, or others whom you would like to provide funds for, this is an ideal way of making that happen.

In addition to these gifts, you can also give gifts of any amount to other causes. This includes giving payments for someone's medical costs or their tuition. You can also give away your property in any amount to tax-exempt charities.

Interest in a family business

In some situations, if you give some minority interest in a family-owned business to someone, this can reduce your taxes. A minority value is less than that of the value of a majority interest, which will keep it undervalued. Because of the minority business discounts that are available, minority interest can be valued much lower.

In addition to this, realize that this tactic will only work for an existing business, not one that you create and place major assets such as your home in. If the business is designed solely to reduce estate taxes, it will not work.

Life insurance

Another way to lower your estate taxes is through life insurance. If you have a life insurance policy at the time of your death, the benefits from the policy will be included in your estate's taxable property. If this policy is large enough and adds too much to your exemption rate, then there could potentially be large amounts of taxes applied to it. On the other hand, if you do not own the policy, but someone else does, the funds are not subject to tax.

In order for this to happen, the gift of insurance must be made at least three years before you die. No deathbed gifts can be made simply because of the potential tax savings.

These gifts are subject to gift taxes. The worth of the policy is the current value of it. This is much less than what is paid at the time of death. In addition, if the present value of that insurance is less than $13,000, once again, there is no tax here.

One way to make this happen is to simply give the policy to another person. You will need an assignment form from your insurance company, or you can use an irrevocable life insurance trust that will transfer ownership to the other person. If you do not have someone specific to transfer funds to, you should consider a life insurance trust.

There are some disadvantages to using this type of gift to avoid estate taxes. If you sign your life insurance over to someone, you no longer can make changes to it. You cannot cancel it, either. Consider how this will affect your needs.

AB Trusts

Next, consider the AB trust. We mentioned it earlier in Chapter 8, but let us go into a bit more detail here. If you are a well-off couple and know that your shared estate property will push you too far over the estate tax threshold in valuation, you may want to consider this trust. While it will not likely wholly avoid estate taxes, it will lower how much is owed in total.

As has been previously discussed, there is a set amount of estate value that you can have before you are pushed over the threshold and must pay taxes on it (subject to changes that may happen under the current Congress and President's administration). Nevertheless, it is important to understand how this will play a role.

Let us say that you leave your estate to your spouse when you die. The value of the living spouse's estate can rise significantly at this time and therefore push them over the threshold and into taxes. This means that the tax will then need to be assessed against your funds as well as theirs when they die. This is sometimes called a second tax. This lowers the total amount that will pass down to your heirs when both spouses are gone.

With an AB trust, you can avoid some of this tax without having to split your property apart from each other when one passes away. In an AB trust, your assets and your spouse's are kept separate, but the surviving spouse is able to use the property in the trust as they need and want to for basic needs and for health care. But they do not gain ownership of that property.

Establishing an AB trust will require the transferring of most or all the property of each spouse into a separate trust. This is often done with the help of a living trust that spans over both spouse's trusts. While you both are alive, the property is in the living trust and can be changed at any time. But there are two separate trusts under the living trust that divide the property between the two spouses. Placing all this property into Trust A is step one.

When one spouse dies, the living trust property is split into two separate trusts. Trust A is the deceased spouse's trust. This trust becomes irrevocable. The other trust is Trust B, which is the surviving spouse's living trust.

This is one of the best ways of managing trusts because there is no way to know which spouse will die first. Both will create a Trust A, but only one will go into action. In the creation of these trusts, the "life beneficiary" of the trust is named as the other spouse. This inclusion allows for the surviving spouse to take use of the property in Trust A for his or her own needs. It does not provide ownership of this property to the spouse, though, which is the key factor in avoiding estate taxes.

In doing this, the life beneficiary has the right to use the property in the trust, to receive all income from the property, and to spend the trust principal for health, support, maintenance, and education as a method of maintaining their current lifestyle.

In addition to this, each spouse will name beneficiaries on his or her AB trust. After both individuals are gone, the final beneficiaries are used to divide property. In addition, there must be a trustee in place that will manage and watch over the trust. In most cases, this will be your spouse. When one spouse dies, an alternative successor is assigned to Trust A and Trust B.

What are the benefits?

An AB trust will work for several key situations. If you want to leave most of your estate to your spouse, it works well. If you have a combined estate with your spouse that is valued over the estate tax threshold, it can be beneficial.

Those who have a good deal of wealth should consider AB trusts. Elderly couples who will likely not outlive each other by many years should also consider them, as they will reduce the amount of estate tax that will need to be paid. Yet, it is important that several key understandings be in place as well for a trust to work.

Both spouses, as well as the final beneficiaries, should understand and agree on the trusts and how they are set up. The goal of a trust is to save money through avoidance of estate taxes and to allow for the surviving spouse to have full use of the property they both own. It is necessary for the entire group to understand the property in the trust is for the surviving spouse's use and benefit above all else. In that, it is important for final beneficiaries to realize that the estate tax reduction will benefit the surviving spouse, not the final property owners.

If the surviving spouse does need to use the funds in the trust to maintain his or her lifestyle or to pay medical bills, the final beneficiaries must agree that this is allowable. For situations in which there will be conflict between the surviving spouse and the final beneficiaries, an AB trust can just make it worse. The surviving spouse has the right to use and benefit from what is left in the trust by their spouse who has died. If the final beneficiaries want the funds to be left alone, this can be cause for conflict.

There are some people who may not benefit from an AB trust. Some do not want to leave a large amount of property to the other spouse, and therefore, they can determine where the property goes in other documentation. Then, there are those who need much more extensive help for their estate plans.

Couples who are middle-aged may also not benefit from it. If the surviving spouse lives many years longer than the other, this could cause a number of problems. Also, couples who have one spouse who is much older than the other might have this problem.

Is this right for you?

There are a few reasons why you might not want to consider AB trusts, even though they seem to provide some of the best estate planning for those with estates over the tax threshold. First, take some time to meet with your attorney to go over the process and the benefits. Both of you should understand what is happening and agree on whether it is the right choice for you. You will also want to consider a few things that may push you away from this type of estate plan.

For example, there will be some limitation on the property that is left behind to the surviving spouse. While they can use it to maintain their current lifestyle and for health and education, they still cannot spend the funds left in the trust any way that they want to. You must be legally allowed to use those funds for the purpose you intend.

Of course, there are fees for these trusts that must be taken into consideration. You will need an estate lawyer, who will draw up what these fees will be. He or she will be required to divide the couple's property as equally as possible, which will take some work. In addition, you will need a tax payer ID for the trust because the surviving spouse will need to file an annual income tax return on the trust.

For many, the hardest part of the process will be to maintain accurate records of the trust and its property. This means that the surviving spouse will need to maintain their own property as well as the property that is in the trust.

When everyone understands the process and the requirements of AB trusts, they can be beneficial to those who are using them, especially as a tax advantage.

Is There Anything Else?

If you are still looking for a few more ways to lower the cost of the estate taxes that you pay, there are just a handful of other options.

QTIP trust

A Qualified Terminable Interest Property (QTIP) trust is one option that you have. This trust does not reduce or stop estate taxes, but it does postpone them. It can be used when an individual estate exceeds the estate tax threshold. Let us say that you die and leave behind an estate exceeding the estate tax threshold. You can leave this behind in the QTIP trust, which will delay the payment of the estate taxes. The benefit of the QTIP trust is simple: It provides for the use of the property by the surviving spouse for life but also qualifies for the marital deduction that we talked about in Chapter 8. That means that when the spouse who creates the trust dies, the property is not taxable. In addition, the QTIP allows the individual creating the trust to choose the final beneficiaries.

The estate tax on this property is assessed when the surviving spouse dies, as it is now part of their property. But what is important to note is that the taxes are assessed based on the value of the assets when the surviving spouse dies, not when the first spouse dies. This could significantly raise the value of the property and therefore cause additional tax requirements.

To consider using a QTIP Trust, talk with your financial planner and estate planning lawyer about the benefits in your specific situation, as this is a complex type of trust that requires in-depth consideration with careful foresight.

Life insurance trusts

A life insurance trust is one that you may set up to help you to avoid estate taxes, but it has to be done in a specific manner. This is an irrevocable trust, meaning that it cannot be changed. The trust will own life insurance that you currently own. By transferring your life insurance to the ownership of the trust, you secure the funds before you die. Because the trust owns the life insurance, and not you, it is not subject to estate taxes when you die, as you do not have ownership of it any longer.

The reason for doing this instead of giving ownership of the life insurance to someone else is simple. There may not be someone whom you trust or want to leave the funds to. This gives you the ability to eliminate risks of ownership or even helps you to keep legal control over the policy while you are still alive.

Yet there are some details that you need to consider if you are to make this happen for yourself. First, a life insurance trust must be considered irrevocable, as this removes your ownership from the trust. If you own it, you pay tax on it. Second, you cannot name yourself as the trustee of the trust. Finally, you must put this type of trust in place at least three years before you die.

Charitable remainder trusts

As mentioned earlier, another option that you have is a charitable remainder trust. In this type of trust, you will make an irrevocable gift of property to a tax-free charity. When you set this type of trust in motion, you will receive a set income from the property that you give while you are alive. In doing this, you secure a lower estate tax as well as a lower income tax. The only catch is that when you die, the property must go to the charity. This will eventually cost you more to donate the property than the tax benefits that you will receive, but if you want the property to go to charity anyway, it can be a positive thing.

Generation skipping trust

Earlier in Chapter 8, we talked about the generation skipping trust and how regulations were put into place to limit the problem of people giving their grandchildren their estate to avoid paying estate taxes on it. But you can set up a generation skipping trust to help manage your funds if you wish.

This is something only those who have a good amount of wealth tend to take advantage of. Nevertheless, if you want to leave a trust for your grandchildren, this trust will establish that. Here, the trust will only pay a set income to your children. When your children die, the funds that are left in the trust are given to the final beneficiaries: your grandchildren.

When you die, the property is still included in your estate. That means that if you have more property that puts you over the estate tax threshold, your estate will pay tax on it. But what it does do is help you avoid the second taxing that would happen when the property is passed to your children and then to your grandchildren.

You are limited as to how much you can leave in this type of trust. If you leave more than what is considered the limit for the year in which you die, there will be stiff tax penalties for the amount over it.

If your children are well-off and do not need the property you plan to leave them, and the property will simply pass to your grandchildren when your children die, this type of trust can limit just how much will be taxed.

Survivorship deeds

Like other methods described here, a survivorship deed can work in a key manner. When you purchase property, the deed is placed in the name of two people. When one of those two die, the other automatically gains full ownership of the property. You can also change a deed to provide this same benefit. The benefit of doing so is simple: When the first individual on the deed dies, the other inherits the property as an owner and therefore avoids probate.

This is a good way of avoiding costs on the property twice — such as when both property owners die. Yet it does not work well unless all property is going to one individual when the other dies. For those who want this property to go to several people, this type of deed will not provide for that. It works best for husband-and-wife situations. To set this type of deed up, talk to your attorney about survivorship deeds and their benefit to your estate plan.

Disclaiming Gifts

Disclaiming gifts may be another way to reduce the amount of taxes that your estate will pay when you die. A disclaimer is not a trust, but works somewhat similarly. A disclaimer is an allowance for the beneficiary to simply decline a gift that is given to them, which can include inheritances. When the beneficiary declines the gift, the gift is then passed to the alternative beneficiary.

The most common reason for disclaiming gifts is as simple as the funds not being needed by the beneficiary. If you stand to inherit $200,000 and are well-off and simply do not need it, you can decline the funds, which would then pass down to the alternative beneficiary. This can help with estate taxes because the funds do not go through estate taxing two times — once when the funds are given to the beneficiary, and again when the beneficiary dies.

With all these methods to reduce the estate tax that will become due on your estate, it is important to establish them with your estate planning attorney, who can drastically help you to reduce the risk of something going wrong in the planning. Trusts can be complicated to plan and structure legally.

CASE STUDY: CHRIS D. CAREY

Laribee & Hertrick, LLP
325 North Broadway
Medina, Ohio 44256
(330) 725-0531
Fax (330) 725-0666
cdcarey@laribee-hertrick.com

People should begin thinking about estate planning when they have children or acquire a significant asset, such as a house. The planning process should increase the likelihood that a person will accomplish his or her estate planning goals and save money in the long run. No one can see the future, but those who start planning early will be better situated for whatever comes their way.

Gifting is a simple, often overlooked, and tax-free way to transfer wealth from one generation to the next. The problem with gifting is that once something has been given away, it is gone. Whether gifting is the right choice for someone depends on his or her financial situation and goals.

Proper planning almost always saves attorney fees and expenses in the future. For instance, if someone dies without a will, his or her property will be distributed pursuant to state law, usually to the closest relatives.

CASE STUDY: CHRIS D. CAREY

Even if that is what the person desired, the administration of the estate will be more expensive and time-consuming because the administrator will be required to post bond. In a will, the testator ordinarily specifies that their executor be permitted to serve without bond. The cost of the bond alone could exceed what it would have cost to do a little advanced planning.

The worst case is this: Elderly owners of a family farm transferred the land to several children without consulting an accountant or their attorney, believing that they were saving money. Their failure to consult with an estate-planning professional cost their children the stepped-up basis on death (that the beneficiary's basis equals the fair market value of the property at the time of the decedent's death) and resulted in a capital gains tax liability that far exceeded the costs of probate and estate tax combined.

Bruton Parish Church, Williamsburg, Virginia

Chapter 10

A Comprehensive Estate Plan: Putting the Insurance Pieces Together

Throughout this book, you have learned a good deal about the estate plan and crafting one that puts into perspective how your assets will be handled after your death. If nothing else, you will be able to understand what is going to happen to everything you have worked so hard to earn. But we have presented estate planning in bits and pieces, as a foundation. Now it is time to help you craft what we call a "comprehensive estate plan," which will put all the pieces together and help you establish the best method for managing what is important to you.

As has been mentioned, you should have in place a team of individuals who can help you throughout the process: your attorney, your financial planner, your accountant, and your insurance provider. Each individual should understand what your goals are and who the other players are. In this and subsequent chapters, we will focus on putting together a plan that will assist you in each of these areas.

To get started, we need to take a close look at insurance — one of the primary areas that many people believe will save their family from taxes and despair after they die. Read through this chapter and understand the basics. Then, schedule a meeting with your insurance agent to talk about the products you have and those that you need to provide your family with the protection they need. We recommend working closely with an insurance agent, rather than just with the company, so that you can talk about your needs with someone who will take the time to understand them. If you do not want to do this, you will need the help of your financial advisor to make sure that what you are doing makes financial sense in the long-term.

Insurance Protection

Insurance provides protection, something that your entire estate plan should provide. It can help in a number of different situations. There are those who die unexpectedly, and that means costly bills, as well as the loss of a wage earner in the family. For those who simply cannot work due to disability, it provides additional protection. In addition, it can help to protect you from lawsuits. For example, car insurance can protect you from a lawsuit should you be involved in an accident, and homeowner's insurance can protect you should someone hurt themselves while in your home.

One thing you should never do is purchase more insurance than you need, but you must have a good understanding of what you need to make that decision.

We need to determine what insurance products you need to consider as far as estate planning is concerned. Insurance can help protect your estate from being unexpectedly taken away — for example, if a lawsuit should be filed against you or you find yourself disabled. Insurance can also provide you with protection for those assets that you do not have just yet but will have in your estate later. Finally, it can increase your assets and add additional savings to your estate. You will need to understand how these three types of insurance are important to your estate's well-being.

Protecting current assets

The first reason to have insurance products is to help protect the assets you have so that you do not lose them. Whatever you currently have that is of some value to you should be insured. Assets lose their value all the time due to a variety of situations, including lawsuits, disability, and car accidents. You need protection against these potential losses. Not having enough insurance coverage will play a role in your estate's value. Just getting sick or into a simple car accident could result in a major asset loss.

Many believe that they are protected from this type of loss because they can just file bankruptcy on the claims against them. Again, this would involve giving up assets that could go to your family later on. Take inventory of what you have and determine its value.

Protecting future assets

It may seem strange to tell you that you need insurance to protect what you do not have, but that is the truth. Here, we are talking about future income insurance. Your insurance agent can work with you to determine how much insurance you will need to sustain your future income. But what you need to consider is why you need it.

You should have enough protection through insurance for several key matters:

- It should provide enough coverage to pay off whatever you owe on your mortgage.

- It should provide enough coverage for your family for five to ten years of lost income. This refers to how much you bring home, including overtime and bonuses.

- It should cover large expenses that you foresee, such as your child's college education.

These aspects are important to note because you want to make sure your family can live the standard of life they are accustomed to without your income. Providing enough coverage can help them make it through while they look for additional ways to make ends meet down the road.

An important note to consider here is stocks and mutual funds. If this is part of your estate, you should consider what type of coverage you need for the losses that can happen there as well. If your estate's value is wrapped up in real property, this too should be taken into consideration.

With life insurance, you need to look into the costs that will be necessary to maintain the current standard of living should you or your family lose your income, either now or after you die.

Insurance for after you die

While insurance products can protect your family and help make ends meet, they can also do more. For example, they can help you level off the gift giving that you will do in your estate plan. If you need additional funds to provide for an equal gift to your loved ones, this may need to be included in the insurance products that you have.

If you feel the need to leave behind a substantial amount of money to someone, a life insurance policy can provide it. But it can be costly to do this because of the monthly or yearly insurance premiums that need to be paid. For this reason, work with your insurance agent to determine the policy that will provide you with the most long-term benefits.

Types of Insurance Coverage

There are many types of insurance products, each with their own specific benefits to you and your family. In estate planning, you need to carefully consider each of them.

Here are a few areas to think about.

Health insurance

Health insurance is something that you might not have thought about in regard to estate planning. But if you do not have some form of health coverage, chances are high that when you do die, there will be expensive medical bills to pay, which could potentially wipe out your estate in the process.

You need health insurance for basic needs such as trips to the doctor's office, but look closer at what happens when something larger and much more expensive happens. Do you have coverage for such things as long-term care, cancer treatment, hospitalization, and rehabilitation? What does your health coverage provide in these cases?

Look at the maximum amounts on your health insurance plan or policy. Some policies have "maximum payment per incident" or "maximum lifetime benefits." These maximum amounts will help define how much your estate can be hit by a large medical bill. For example, if your policy only covers 70 percent of the medical bills per incident, that leaves a potential 30 percent behind that someone has to pay, which would come from your estate. This would be a highly expensive bill if, say, you were to suffer a heart attack and needed long-term rehabilitation. In your estate plan, you must take into account the potential for large costs that your health insurance will not cover.

The solution to these costs is not to set aside some funds for them, but to provide yourself with adequate health insurance to cover them. Having 100 percent coverage will provide you and your family with peace of mind knowing that if something happens, the bills are paid in full.

Disability income insurance

With disability income insurance, you provide protection in case something happens to you and you are unable to work or earn an income. Many people do not take this type of insurance as seriously as they should, but disability can happen for many reasons.

Unlike life insurance, disability insurance provides you with protection from being unable to earn an income while you are still alive. You can purchase disability coverage if it is not provided to you by your employer, which is often the case. There are two main types to consider.

- **Short-term**: Short-term disability provides you coverage for a period of three months or longer and is provided to you when you use your current or future vacation balance.
- **Long-term**: In comparison, long-term coverage is provided for a longer length of time, most often for many years, and will replace your income or a large part of it.

When considering the purchase of disability insurance, it is essential to consider what the policy is providing. One thing to consider is what percentage of coverage it provides. Some policies limit this quite substantially.

Obviously, you want as much as you can get. Some policies allow you to choose which percentage is right for you.

Another consideration is the "cost of living adjustment," which means that payments will adjust for inflation over the time the policy is used — a crucial feature. Also, consider how long the disability coverage will pay out. Some policies stop paying when you hit retirement age and begin to receive social security from the federal government.

Disability insurance can help protect your estate, too. It provides you with the means to make money when you otherwise could not. Those who find themselves unable to work and without this type of insurance can lose virtually all that they own due to the costs of living. Protecting your estate means having enough coverage to provide you with an income in nearly any situation.

Long-term care insurance

Catastrophic illness can happen to anyone at any time. Some of the most disturbing and shocking news that we hear is of a completely healthy person being diagnosed with a catastrophic illness. Long-term medical treatment can be one of the most expensive matters a family can face, and you need some method of paying for it. In comes long-term care insurance, which may protect you against this type of medical expense.

Whereas disability coverage protects you from losing your ability to provide income for your family, long-term care insurance provides you with protection from the expenses that go along with the illness or accident recovery you might face. Because it is nearly impossible for you to determine when and if this will happen to you, you have two choices to consider. You can put some money away in your estate plan to pay for long-term care (which may push you over the allowable limit to avoid estate taxes if it is not used) and hope that it is enough, or you can invest in long-term care insurance.

Many people end up in assisted living facilities because their spouse and children cannot take care of them on an ongoing basis in their home. You may even dictate in your estate plan what your wishes in these situations are. Nevertheless, a nursing home, a long-term assisted living facility, or in-home care needs to be paid for.

When planning for long-term care insurance, make sure that it will work with your disability insurance. With your insurance agent, determine what your needs are in terms of amount of coverage, as well as what may be covered by the disability insurance that you purchase. In addition, determine how well the long-term care insurance works in relation to the health-care coverage that you have. You want to make sure that coverage extends throughout your time of need, without any lapses in coverage, which could cost your estate a considerable amount of money.

With the help of your insurance agent, determine the right amount of health care coverage for your needs. Without this type of long-term care insurance or some other method of paying for it, your estate must pay for the cost of your long-term care needs. If there is no method to pay for this, your estate could be drained of value in order to pay for these needs.

Auto insurance

All types of insurance are important to your estate plan, including auto insurance. With this type of coverage, there are several key areas to think about. First, you simply should never drive a car that does not have coverage according to Virginia's laws. Without proper insurance, a simple traffic accident could cost you thousands of dollars in damages, lawsuits, and fines — if not more.

Second, look at the type of auto insurance policy that you have. The most important consideration is that of liability coverage. Does the policy limit you on a per-person or per-incident basis? If there is a limit in this regard, it could cost you a considerable amount of money.

The best route to take in planning your estate is to talk with your insurance agent about what types of auto insurance you need, how much you need, and what type of limitations are on the coverage. In most cases, they will help you determine, based on your specific situation, what your needs are. You should always have plenty of auto insurance for all your vehicles.

Homeowner's insurance

Like auto insurance, homeowner's (and renter's) insurance is a product that you should have. If you have a mortgage, you have to have homeowner's insurance; the lender will require it. But even if your home is paid in full and you think you can rebuild the entire house on the funds that you have, you should still have homeowner's insurance.

Again, there is one word that you need to consider: liability. The main reason to have homeowner's insurance is for protection from the loss of your home, yet it also should provide you with adequate liability coverage. Let us say that someone comes into your home and is hurt when your large television falls on them. Not only might they sue you for injury and medical damages, but what if they can no longer work? What if they win a claim of mental anguish? Here, there is the potential for a serious amount of cost to you and your home. Plenty of people end up losing their homes — not to mention other estate property — in the process of these lawsuits. Working with your insurance agent, determine what the worst liability issue that could happen to you is and plan for it in your estate plan. Adequate homeowner's insurance is crucial.

Umbrella liability

We just talked about the importance of liability coverage with auto and homeowner's coverage. Yet, chances are you do not have enough coverage with those policies. Although this sounds dismal, it is a simple fact: The more valuable your estate is, the more likely it is that someone will go after you for a larger amount of money. It only takes one auto accident or one fall on your property to hurt you in terms of your estate's value without the right amount of coverage.

For this reason, many insurance agents suggest using an umbrella policy to provide additional coverage for any type of liability claim against you. This extends further than any other liability that you have, providing you with much more coverage.

Work with your insurance agent to determine the best coverage for you. A good insurance agent can help you figure out whether you need umbrella liability coverage, how much you need, and what is too much. Decide on the worst-case scenario and work from there.

Life insurance

We have saved life insurance coverage for last because it is complex and should be taken quite seriously.

When you die, life insurance pays a significant amount of money to your beneficiaries. That is the simple explanation of what life insurance is; you will find that it gets a bit more complex as we move on. There are a number of important reasons to have a life insurance policy in place that will pay out to beneficiaries when you die.

Here are some reasons why you need to consider life insurance as part of your estate plan:

1. **It will help replace the income that you bring into the family unit when you die.** This benefit can be immensely important to your family whom you leave behind.

2. **It provides liquidity.** That means that when you die, the funds are easily accessible. For people who have value that is mostly in real estate or other assets, getting cash to their survivors will be important. Life insurance can provide that ability.

3. **Estate taxes can be covered.** You can use your life insurance policy to help your survivors pay estate taxes. Though eliminating estate taxes is nearly impossible, providing funds to cover them is not that difficult when you can use a life insurance policy to do it.

4. **It can pay off the debt that you leave behind.** If you have debt in any form, you can use your life insurance policy to pay it off when you die. This removes the requirement that your survivors find the funds to pay off what you owe.

The preceding list is a basic look at what life insurance can provide you, but if you have spoken with your insurance agent at this point, you also know that there are a handful of different options for you to consider. This is where it can get complex if you do not have a handle on the right insurance product for your needs.

First, determine whether you need life insurance. If you need to provide for any of the preceding benefits to your family, you need it. If you do not need to provide these, you might not need it, or might not need an extensive policy.

Next, determine what term your life insurance needs to provide. Long-term insurance is important in some cases. But in others, term life insurance, which only extends for a time period, might be all that is needed. For example, you might need term life insurance until you are no longer working because at that point, you are not earning an income that needs to be protected anymore. On the other hand, most people carry some debt throughout their life, so long-term life insurance may be necessary to pay this debt off in the event of your death.

Now, let us look at several key types of life insurance and what they can provide to you. Work with your insurance agent to define what you need and determine what you will benefit from the most.

Whole life insurance

This is the only type of life insurance many people know about. Whole life insurance is a straightforward plan. You make premium payments over the time of the insurance product, and part of that payment will go into a special account that earns interest. It develops a cash value over time that can even be borrowed against while you have the insurance in effect. What is more, should you cancel your policy, you get the cash proceeds that are being "saved" for you back.

Universal life insurance

Just like whole life insurance, universal life insurance provides you with a guaranteed return on your investment. This type of insurance became popular when interest rates and inflation were high in the '80s, but is still available. The potential benefit it provides, in contrast to that of whole life, is a higher rate of return. Your policy will provide you with details on what specifically it will potentially return to you. Like whole life insurance, it does provide you with a cash value over time.

Variable life insurance

With variable life insurance, you take some control over where your money is invested. Some people have more of a risk threshold and want their funds to earn more by putting them in the stock market. Others feel safer with bonds. Yet the potential here to benefit can be high and risky. In some cases, you can lose a considerable amount of money, like when the stock market plummets.

Term life insurance

The biggest difference between whole life insurance policies and term life insurance policies is that term products do not have any cash value while you are alive; not until you die will they pay out. The other difference is that if the policy is no longer in effect, it pays nothing, even when you die. It is for a specific term or length of time.

Term life insurance is offered by a wide range of insurance companies, and there are plenty of different plans to choose from. One that you may encounter is called "annual renewal term policies." With this type of product, your death benefits do not increase, but when you are younger, your premiums are adjusted yearly. Then, you have those policies that "lock" you into a specific premium for a set amount of time, meaning that during that time, the premium does not go up or down. Finally, you have those policies that provide for "decreasing term" insurance. Here, the premium payments will stay the same over the entire policy period, but the death benefits go down as you age.

Company-provided life insurance

Your employer may provide you with some or all your life insurance. Many companies offer this type of incentive as a benefit to working there. Yet not all policies are the same. Talk with your human resources manager about what policies they have for you, what they include, and what they provide. Do not assume that if you have a $250,000 life insurance policy through your job, it is a straight life insurance policy.

One type of insurance product offered through employers is a "key person life insurance policy." This insurance is provided for the highest-ranking individuals in the company. If you own a business, you might have this coverage for yourself, too. Another type is called "split dollar life insurance." This type of insurance provides for a more complex situation that is used to provide insurance for several of the company's high ups. If you have this type of policy, it is important to find out from your human resources manager exactly what it is providing you.

For those who do not hold the top positions within a company, which would be most, do not worry — there is likely life insurance available to you through the company. Sometimes, employees do not realize they have it. What is more, you may have the ability to obtain it in larger amounts if you purchase extra coverage through your company. For some, this type of insurance is limited to only cover your death if you die while working for the company or traveling for the company. Again, you need to find out from your human resources manager what you have and what you can purchase in addition to that.

Life Insurance and Taxes

There are taxes on your life insurance, and you need to know what to expect so that you can plan for it in your estate plan. In some cases, those who have the ability to control their life insurance policies find that the value of those policies can be added into the value of their estate, therefore pushing their estate's value higher.

As we mentioned earlier, estate taxes come into play when your estate is valued higher than the allowable limit — the estate tax threshold. Now, before you begin to write off life insurance as part of your estate, consider several factors. First, unless you go over the estate tax limit for the year that you die, you will not have to pay any taxes on life insurance. These limits change from year to year, so check with your attorney to determine what this is likely to be in coming years.

The good news is that even if you do go over the allowable amount, there are several key ways that you can avoid taxes on your life insurance. We touched on this in earlier chapters, but let us go into a bit more detail.

If you transfer the ownership of your life insurance policy to someone else, then you no longer own it, and therefore, it cannot be considered part of your estate. Unless it is part of your estate, it cannot be taxed when you die. Yet the key here is that once you sign it over to someone else, you lose control of it. You cannot change your beneficiaries, you cannot cancel your policy, and you cannot otherwise manage the policy. Another drawback here is that you can potentially be required to pay gift taxes or federal estate taxes when you transfer the funds to someone else.

The other option that you have to help you avoid estate taxes for your insurance policy is that of an irrevocable life insurance trust. Here, you will give up control of your life insurance policy, but you do not have to consider the death benefit being included into your estate's value for taxation.

One key element to realize is this: You cannot make changes to your life insurance policy like this (transferring ownership) and see benefits if you die within three years of doing so. The government has limited the transferring of life insurance to avoid estate taxes to three years prior to your death so that you cannot change these terms on your deathbed. If you plan to make these changes, do it sooner rather than later.

Check with your financial planning team to make sure that you understand the tax implications that could affect you here. Determine what the best way is to avoid the taxes that you are facing with life insurance. This is a collective effort. Your insurance agent is likely to just sell you as much life insurance as you need. But, with the help of your financial planner, your accountant, and your attorney, you can determine the tax implications on purchasing that level of insurance.

Balance the amount of life insurance that you have with the amount allowable without pushing your estate's value over the threshold and therefore causing it to be taxed. Ultimately, you need to make sure that having too much life insurance does not hurt your estate plan.

Summing It Up

Now that you know what life insurance can and cannot provide you, consider what this means for your needs.

1. **If the worst happened to you, what would it do to your family financially?** What type of insurance product do you need to provide coverage for you and your family and to what degree? Weigh the worst-case scenario with the cost of the policies that you are considering.

2. **What is at risk?** If you do not have enough coverage of any type, what could you and your family lose in the process? In many cases, this might well be everything that you have, including your home. Determine, with the help of your attorney, what the most is that can be taken from you through the laws of Virginia.

3. **How long do you need the coverage?** Some forms of insurance only need to be held for a period of time. Others are needed over the lifetime that you are in possession of them. Determine the right length of coverage per insurance product by discussing options with your insurance provider and adjust it to make the most sense in your life and estate plan.

On a final note, you might want to find out about other protections that are available to you through Virginia state government. At present, Virginia offers services to those qualified for assistance through Medicaid and also Virginia's Family Access to Medical Insurance Security (FAMIS) program. Both are focused for relative low-income assistance, with FAMIS targeted only for children. For FAMIS eligibility information, see: **www.famis.org/eligibility.cfm?lang=English**.

For example, some long-term medical coverage can be provided to you through these governmental programs. As we mentioned, your family may need to pay this back as part of the Estate Recovery Act out of your estate when you die. Note that insurance coverage options are under consideration of Congress as this book goes to press. Changes at the federal and/or state level are likely to occur in the near future.

Insurance is a key factor in your estate plan. For many, it helps to provide for the connection, and ultimately for the funding, of several key aspects of your estate. Whatever you use it for, make sure that you weigh the cost of the insurance, the benefits it provides, and the reward that it will provide to those you leave behind. For most people, some life insurance and other insurance products are immeasurably beneficial to their financial well-being, both before and after they die.

Captain Smith Statue, Jamestown, Virginia

Chapter 11

Planning for Long-Term Care

In previous chapters, we have touched on some important topics in relation to planning what will happen to your estate once you die. It is also important to consider some aspects in your estate plan that might come into play before you die. Now that you have a good understanding of the products available to help you throughout the planning of your will, it is important for you to consider the long-term care needs, medical requirements, and financial decisions that must be made. Much of this will be taken care of with your will, as we have talked about. Yet you need to ultimately define what your wishes are so that they can be carried out in full.

It Will Not Happen to Me

One of the greatest problems you might have is the mentality that nothing bad can or will happen to you. There is ultimately no way to predict what the future holds. As you age, your body becomes more at risk for both physical and mental challenges. While you are in a good position, you need to make decisions for the "what if" situations that could potentially happen to you.

If you do become mentally challenged in the future, such as with Alzheimer's or another limiting disease or condition, you will not be able to make the right decisions for yourself or your estate. It might fall on your next in line if you do not make these decisions now. Even if you do pull through from these conditions, then in the end, it can still hold you at the mercy of those who have been forced to make decisions for you, such as your spouse, your children, or others.

At any age and in any health situation, you should have these basic considerations laid out so that in the untimely situation of your death or illness, there is no doubt what your desires are.

To help you do this, let us talk about several key aspects in caring for yourself and your family that you should have written down.

Medical Decisions to Consider

How do you feel about your life being prolonged by a machine? There are two thoughts to this. Some do not want a machine to keep them alive at a potentially high cost when they feel that there will be no benefit in the end. For others, the chance that they will recover is enough for them to want this type of treatment used. There are all types of methods that can be used to prolong your life through medical devices and services. Only you know how you feel about these situations.

In recent years, the Supreme Court has ruled that patients have the right to die with dignity. They have the right to not go through painful, overly stressful, and highly expensive treatments that can prolong their life artificially. Every state has also confirmed this right.

If you do not make this decision, you put it in the hands of those who love you. Will they be in any real condition to make this choice for you?

Will they regret the choice that they make years later? Wi
whether they made the right choice for the rest of their li
the decision, you lessen the requirements and the stress
family during an already difficult time.

Once you have made the decision about your wishes, which is something that you should talk about with your closest loved ones, you should put this in writing. Each of the states, including Virginia, has put in place an allowable, simple document that any person can complete to help determine what these wishes are.

You will need to prepare at least two types of documents to make your wishes known:

- **Declaration**: This is a written statement that tells doctors and health care personnel what your specific wishes are regarding various types of treatments. This is also called an "advance directive" or a "living will." A living will does not leave property or other possessions through it, but spells out your medical wishes to medical personnel.

- **Durable power of attorney**: This second document selects one person to be responsible for making sure that your wishes are carried out. This person is also called an "Attorney in Fact." This person can also have a variety of other responsibilities if you wish them to, including:

    – Power to hire or discharge medical personnel as needed.

    – Access to your medical records, including all your personal information, most often to help make decisions for you.

- Right to visit you at the facility where you are, even when other visiting is restricted.
- Power to get court authorization to enforce your wishes, such as giving or withholding the treatment that you have requested in your living will or advance directive.

Sometimes, a durable power of attorney is given a specific health care proxy, which is a statement by you giving the person the right to make medical decisions for you. As described here, this works the same as an attorney in fact would. A health care proxy is simply another term for this right and is the recommended approach in Virginia.

One of the most important details that you need to determine here is who the right person will be to have the durable power of attorney over your situation. This person should be someone who is likely to be close enough to your residence to be able to quickly make decisions as necessary. Indeed, the person must be willing to provide this for you, which may mean extensive care at the hospital or other situations. They should also be someone whom you can trust to carry out your decisions and not be swayed or convinced otherwise. Family and doctors can often try to influence a decision one way or another. Finally, the person must be someone who can understand your medical situation and make decisions based on this information.

Some states have requirements on who can and cannot be your attorney in fact or durable power of attorney or advanced medical directive. For example, most states do not allow doctors to hold this position. In Virginia, the limitations are against a witness being a spouse or blood relative. Also, note that as long as you are of sound mind, you can change your decisions anytime that you need or want to.

Finally, you need to decide what directions to state in your living will. The good news is that you do not have to be a medical professional to make these decisions, but you should educate yourself on your options. In your declaration, consider making decisions about these things:

- **Cardiopulmonary resuscitation (CPR)**: Do you want them to try and restart your heart? To what length?
- **Respirators**: Do you want them to keep your body breathing through machines?
- **Surgery**: Do you want them to take any and all means necessary through surgery to try to improve your situation?
- **Medications**: Do you want medications administered to you to reduce the amount of pain that you are in? Do you want medications that can make you more comfortable in your last hours or days?
- **Feeding tubes**: Do you want doctors to provide food and water to you through artificial means, such as through feeding tubes, when you cannot eat on your own?
- **Blood**: Do you want blood or other blood-related products administered to you as needed?
- **Testing**: Do you want all possible tests run on you, such as diagnostic tests?
- **Dialysis**: Do you wish for the doctors to use dialysis on you in critical situations?
- **Drugs and antibiotics**: Do you want these administered to you when you are in a critical situation?

When you look at these questions, you need to consider them thoroughly. In what circumstances do you want these treatments to be used, and when should they not be used? Do you want to make your decisions known here in your declaration or living will, or do you want to leave the decisions to your attorney in fact? Of course, for those with long-term disabling conditions, the decisions might be quite different than for those who are relatively healthy and end up in a critical condition. If you are planning your living will or other similar directives while you already have a long-term condition, you may be more aware of specific wishes you would like carried out.

The foregoing discussion explains the considerations and the various ways you might arrange for your affairs and your personal health matters to be controlled according to your wishes in those situations where you are unable to assert yourself, or make decisions in the way you would wish for yourself. As noted, each state has laws that cover specifically how you can handle these concerns in advance.

Many people who have executed living wills do not realize these documents will not necessarily prevent the administration of CPR in emergency situations unless a separate order is in place that is somehow able to be communicated to emergency responders. Even then, such an order is not going to be issued or followed unless a person is already in such a debilitative, poor state of health that such measures are unlikely to be successful under any circumstances. It is the do not resuscitate (DNR) order and other advanced health care directives that will become effective after emergency measures are past. If you are certain about your instructions for every possible medical scenario, it is important that you fully inform medical personnel, your lawyer, and your family to ensure that your instructions are followed according to your wishes.

Virginia pulls these concepts together in a suggest form of written advance directives set forth in Virginia Code section 54.1-2984. Please refer to Appendix A for a complete copy of this form. An advance directive executed pursuant to this article may, but need not, be in the form. Note there are various options to consider in selection.

When they go into effect

It is important for you to understand when your documents will go into effect. In most cases, there are three situations in which this can happen:

1. You are diagnosed with a terminal condition, or you are in a permanent state of comatose.

2. You cannot communicate for some reason about the medical care that you need. This refers to situations where you cannot communicate in writing, orally, or through gestures.

3. When medical personnel are told that you have written directives for your medical care, they go into effect. In some cases, this information can be placed in your hospital or other medical records so that they will know what your wishes are from the start of treatment.

This might be important for those who find themselves in situations where they are facing long-term illness or conditions that might affect their mental capacity down the road.

You should work closely with your attorney to establish a living will and durable power of attorney as soon as possible. It can and should become part of your estate. You should notify the person whom you want to be your attorney in fact and make sure they agree to make the decisions that you have set forth. Give copies of your living will to several key people to make sure that someone has it when the time comes.

To help you make decisions regarding your life sustaining efforts, use research, specialty doctors, and your regular physician to help you.

Finalize your health-care decisions

Now that you have your documents created, you need to have them finalized, which is an easy process. Each state has its own special requirements, which your attorney can help you with. But you will need to sign your documents, as this will show that you agree to them and that they are your wishes. You will need witnesses or a notary to be present when you sign them. Those who are present must be able to state that you were of sound mind when making these decisions and that you were over the age of 18.

Give your finalized documents to:

- Your attorney in fact;
- Your doctor with whom you work regularly or the one who is handling your health situations currently;
- The health care facility that you commonly use, including the hospital where you are most likely to be treated;
- Any other people who are important to you and who should be made aware of your situation and your decisions.

Final Arrangements

Perhaps one of the most challenging things for people to consider is their own mortality. Yet when you are planning your estate, you should consider the final arrangements that you need and want at the time of your death.

You can do this in your estate plan. It can help to ease tensions and stress on your family. Planning out your wishes in your estate plan can also help to alleviate the costs of your final arrangements.

The important questions to answer are these:

1. What do you want done with your body when you die?
2. What religious ceremonies and other ceremonies do you want?

Only you can say what you want to happen here. If you leave all these decisions for family members, it is important to realize both the emotional strain and the financial strain that it can cause for them. When you make plans now, you might even be able to make final arrangements more affordably than if they were done at the time of your death.

Any and all aspects of your final arrangements should be spelled out for your loved ones in your own wishes. You should consider special instructions, too. Here are a few details to think about:

- Do you want a traditional or religious funeral service? This tends to include the embalming of the body, the resources of a funeral home, and the cremation or burial of your body.

- Do you want a simple funeral service that does not include embalming? Sometimes individuals would rather have a memorial service or even independent arrangements made for them.

- Will you donate your body to a medical school or for other scientific research? If so, you will need to make arrangements for this with the organization you plan to donate to ahead of time. In most cases, once the body has been used for medical study, it is then cremated.

- Do you want to donate any livable organs from your body? Giving to an organ bank should be set up beforehand or should be entrusted to your attorney in fact. Once your body has donated these organs, the rest of the body will go to whomever you designate to take it in order to be buried or cremated as you wish.

- Do you have other wishes that you would like to express for your funeral, your burial, or the manner in which your body is treated?

As with your medical decision documents, you should have your final arrangements declared in a written statement, with all the same information provided. Do not include this information in your will, as your will is not likely to be read until well after your funeral. The document that you create must be readily available at the time of your death, or even right beforehand.

Making Financial Decisions

Just as in the case of medical decisions, you also should spell out your needs and wishes for the financial decisions that must be made. Often people get into a position where they no longer can communicate what their wishes are, and when it comes to money, there tends to be a number of people trying to get it.

Just as you have created a set of documents for the medical decisions that you wish, you should do the same for financial decisions that arise when you no longer can make your own wishes known. This involves the use of a durable power of attorney, who is someone that you leave your financial needs in the hands of. Again, this person is called your attorney in fact and makes decisions for you based on the wishes that you set forth when you do have the ability to do so, and every state in the Union recognizes these types of documents.

If you do not appoint someone to make these decisions for you, then when the situation arises, those who wish to help you make those decisions regarding your finances must get court-appointed power of attorney, which may be in your best interest. The procedure to make this happen is called conservatorship or guardian proceedings. Of course, if you simply plan for this outright by creating a durable power of attorney, you forgo this potentially complex proceeding.

When creating this documentation, you have the same basic abilities as you do when creating a durable power of attorney for your medical decisions — which can be the same person, if you so wish. You will appoint the attorney in fact as well as outline the financial decisions that you want him or her to take on when you no longer can do so. You can limit this quite a bit, or you can allow them to make whatever decision seems to be the best in your situation.

As you can tell, a crucial element of this proceeding will be having a large amount of trust in the person that you are appointing here. You need to know that he or she will do what you have decided, not what the person personally believes is beneficial to you. Realize that this person only has the financial power that you grant them in the document, no more and no less. In general, most attorneys in fact have the ability to make standard payments and deposits for you, such as in an effort to keep your household running. Anything beyond this is something that you should spell out in the documentation.

While it is important for you to take into consideration any and all financial situations and the decisions that you want the attorney in fact to make, you will not be able to predict everything that could possibly happen. In these cases, you will need to know that the person behind you as your attorney in fact is someone you absolutely trust to make decisions for you.

What should you have them do?

In most cases, people who write up durable power of attorneys for financial decisions will allow them control over much of their finances. Some items that you should think about are:

- Management of your retirement accounts
- Operation of your small business and business interests
- Use of your assets to make payments for expenses in everyday living
- Making payments for your family as needed
- Handling real estate that you own or will own — such as buying and selling it, maintaining it, and paying taxes on it — and handling other property that you own
- Handling the benefits that you receive from such things as social security, governmental programs, military service, pensions, and Medicare
- Investing the funds that you have as you wish them to be invested, such as in stocks and bonds or mutual funds
- Working with your financial institutions
- Paying taxes and filing your yearly taxes

These are just a few of the situations in which you will want to consider having someone make decisions for you. You might have other needs that must be met when it comes to financial matters.

Once you have an idea of what you wish to include in these documents, work with your attorney to set up this durable power of attorney in the same manner that your durable power of attorney for medical decisions has been set up. Both purposes can be served in one document if you wish. However, if this is not the same person for both jobs, make sure they can work together when the time comes. Consult an attorney about your options.

When to put them into effect

Now that you have defined your needs and concer cial matters, you need to put them into effect. Fi is easy to do, just as we described in medical dec provide this document to those who should have a copy, including your attorney in fact, your attorney, and those close to you.

You can decide when this document will go into effect. You can file the documents to go into effect immediately, such as when you have been diagnosed with a condition that will leave you mentally unable to make these decisions, or you can make them go into effect when your doctor says that you are incapacitated and no longer can make decisions for yourself. If you choose the latter route, which is called a "springing power of attorney," you should realize that your attorney in fact will have to prove that you are incapacitated by getting statements from doctors. Even then, it can be hard for them to gain control of your finances.

Another action that you can take is to trust the attorney in fact to only take over your finances when you no longer can do so, even though you give him or her immediate control over them. Of course, you should trust them when you appoint them to this position; otherwise, they should not be there.

Often, this is a worrisome matter for people, as handing over their financial situation might be risky to them. Therefore, you should make these decisions carefully and only after you have talked to all involved and feel confident in your decisions.

If you have any concerns about what will happen to you when you are unable to make decisions for yourself, or you have any worries about what will happen when you die, spell out your wishes in documentation and appoint an attorney in fact to manage these wishes.

Colonial House, Williamsburg, Virginia

Chapter 12

Your Estate Plan and Your Retirement Money

Your estate plan is nearly complete. You have filtered into it where you want all your real property to go; you know how you want the last years of your life to play out. Now, you need to factor in anything else that might contribute to the value of your estate or even to those last years. Your retirement income should be considered and planned for in your estate. This will likely take some time to make happen, and it will depend on what goals you have for the current and leftover funds when you die.

First, Invest

What tax-deferred accounts are there that you can invest in? Tax deferred simply means that when you invest your dollars this way, taxes are not paid at that time. Before you can have money to plan for your retirement, you have to first put it in tax-deferred accounts. No matter what age you currently are, it is essential to plan for retirement in some form.

Here are a few of the tax-deferred accounts that you should consider — with the help of your financial planner:

- Individual retirement account (IRA)
- 401(k) accounts
- Keogh plan, which is used for the self-employed

In these types of accounts, dollars invested are not taxed at the time of investment, but when the funds come out during retirement. For example, if your employer has a 401(k) account set up for the company, you can invest pre-tax dollars into it through payroll deductions. The funds enter the account and, ideally, continue to rise in value, without being levied any taxes until the funds come out. For this reason, these accounts are called tax-deferred. Later in this chapter, we will explore how each of these can impact your estate plan.

Your financial planner can help you choose the right investments based on your short-term and long-term goals here.

Into Your Estate Plan

Here, we will talk about planning for any retirement money that you have and how to position it in your estate plan for the most benefit. Retirement money includes funds that you have in an IRA or in 401(k) plans. You may have a pension plan or other plans that have helped you save money for your retirement. Individuals often put these funds away so that when they stop working, they have funds to live off. Because you may not spend it all before you die, you need to figure it into your estate plan.

When you do die, whatever is left over in these accounts is factored in as part of your estate value, which means it could ultimately determine whether you pay estate tax.

Most people will need to make a single decision about their retirement funds before they move forward. That is, what exactly are you saving the funds in your "retirement" accounts for? Some will use this money to fund their retirement, meaning that the amount is used for day-to-day expenses. For others, they use other property to fund their retirement and keep these accounts for their estate for after they die. Let us explore how each of these situations can affect you.

To pay for retirement

Let us say that you are using your retirement funds to pay for your retirement years. Here, you are not worried about leaving these funds behind, but using them throughout your retirement years as you need and want to. In this situation, you still have specific goals for what will happen to what is left over, but that is just it: It is only for what is left over.

If you want to use these accounts for this purpose, you need to work closely with your financial advisor to plan for this. They will use a variety of formulas to help you determine exactly what you need in terms of investments to make this happen. They will look at the accounts that you have and their earnings on an annual basis, your current age, and when you plan to retire, as well as the type of lifestyle you want to live during your retirement years.

As part of your estate plan, work with your financial advisor to determine what the best course of action is so that you have the amount of money that you will need to ultimately pay for the type of retirement lifestyle you will live. In doing this, you are not worried about leaving these funds to your beneficiaries.

To leave behind in an estate plan

For others, retirement accounts are tied to your estate plan. You want to find the right level of living a comfortable retirement but still be able to leave behind funds for your beneficiaries.

When you want your retirement funds to be linked to your estate plan, you will need to work with your financial advisor to link what you are leaving behind to your estate plan. It is no easy job, but one that should be done.

Planning for Your Retirement Funds

As part of the process of establishing your estate plan, we have talked about a number of details under the assumption that you want to leave behind property and an estate for your heirs. If you do not want to do this, then you should work with your financial advisor so that you can develop a plan to use up most of your retirement and other estate valued property while you are alive so that little to nothing is left behind. But most people do want to leave something behind, and for that, we consider the estate plan.

There are many different things to consider in linking your retirement funds to your estate plan. This includes:

- Your pension;
- Your social security benefits;
- Your 401(k);
- Your IRA;
- Other retirement-oriented accounts, such as an employer profit-sharing plan.

Look at your retirement accounts and determine which is the right way for you to link them into your estate plan for the maximum benefit.

Pension accounts

A pension is a post-retirement benefit that an employee receives from an employer after retirement. If you have a pension account, which is becoming rarer these days, you need to consider how it ties into your retirement needs. When you do have one, they are likely to be a significant part of your estate planning. There are two areas to consider with them: You need to look into a contingency plan, and you need to also analyze the estate tax implications that they have in regard to lump sum payments.

Contingency plans

Is your pension insured? If you do not know, you need to find out through your human resources manager. If it is insured, you also need to know how much of it is insured. As frequently seen in the last years, many people can lose their pensions as a result of a company going under because of a scandal.

You should determine whether your pension has coverage through the Pension Benefit Guarantee Corporation (PBGC) of the federal government. This agency provides partial or complete protection to some pensions, but not to all. For example, those who have a pension plan through a professional service firm, like a doctor or law firm, are not insured through this agency if they have under a certain amount of employees. Church pension plans are not insured, nor are pension plans for a government employee. The only way to know whether these plans are insured is to talk with your human resources manager about them.

Along with this information, you need to find out how much it is insured for, as many plans will not be insured to their full value. For some who receive payments before they reach the legal retirement age, these guaranteed amounts of your pension can be lower. If the pension plan includes a survivor or another beneficiary, these can also be lowered as a result. Regardless of whether you have a pension plan insured through PBGC or through your company, you need to know all that you can about this plan in regard to how safe it is to count on for your estate.

When you know how much is guaranteed, you can plan for it. If some or all of it is at risk of being absorbed in the failing of a company, you may want to consider other retirement vehicles to help provide you with the funds that you will need during your retirement years.

Tax implications of lump-sum payments

The other consideration is that of tax implications of payments of a lump sum from your pension plan. Some pensions offer a lump-sum payment at the time of death — which would forgo the rest of your monthly payments — or at a certain point in the future. Indeed, you will still receive your monthly payments, as these tend to be made in addition to those monthly payments. You can find out from your human resources manager whether any lump sum payments are likely to affect you.

You need to understand the tax implications as well as the effect that lump sums can have on your estate plan. For most, it means working with your financial planner to determine the right course of action for this situation.

Estate planning and your pension: What to look at

There are several key things to take into consideration in regard to your estate plan and how your pension will work with it.

First, consider how well your expenses will be covered by your pension payments during your retirement years. You need to cover your expenses in regard to your housing, food, bills, and health care needs. The goal here is to make sure you have enough to live off of but also to plan for you to leave behind an estate for your heirs down the road. Therefore, you will need to consider whether this is your goal.

You may want to spend your entire pension on these needs without regard to leaving anything behind from your pension. That means that this is all that you will need to make sure that your pension covers. Other property may be given away over your lifetime, or you may leave some behind for beneficiaries.

If your plan allows you to have more than enough in pension income to pay your bills, you can use these extra funds as you see fit. But if your pension plan does not provide for enough funds to cover your living expenses, you may need to consider a plan called a "draw down," which will slowly work into your other assets and then cover your bills in the process of doing so.

If you do have an excess amount, this will then be added to your estate. For some, especially those who live modestly, it could push them into a higher tax bracket for estate tax; therefore, you should consider the best way to handle these funds to avoid those taxes.

As we mentioned, pensions are continuously at risk for company failure and corruption, which could put your living expense dollars at risk. For this reason, you do need a backup plan. It could be as simple as drawing from your savings account or other estate holdings to meet living expenses. If you find that you can no longer meet the needs of your estate plan with the reduction of your pension amount, you may need to revisit your estate plan and make adjustments to it to ultimately fix this problem.

Do not forget about inflation, either. Many do, and that could mean a serious problem later on. Find out first whether your pension plan offers some type of inflation compensation, such as an increase in your pension payment based on inflation. If not, you need to again determine a backup plan.

Social security

Social security is complex. As you are still working and earning funds, you might hate to see the large deduction from your paycheck that goes toward social security. Yet in the back of your mind, you likely wonder whether the funds will be available by the time you get there. Depending on where you are in life, this could be a real worry, or something that you do not think about.

Nevertheless, it is important to factor social security into your estate plan, as well as what it will provide to you over the course of your retirement years. For many, it becomes the mainstay of these years.

There are several types of social security:

- **Social security retirement payments**: What most people think of when they think of social security is this payment that they will get once they retire at the federal retirement age — which, by the way, changes based on when you were born.

- **Disability benefits**: If you are hurt or disabled and can no longer work, you may qualify for disability benefits through social security. These can help you make important payments that will safeguard your assets — such as your home.

- **Survivor benefits**: This is a type of benefit that is paid to the surviving family members when you die. A spouse may receive it, or a child under 18 may receive it for their deceased parent.

- **Supplemental security income**: These are funds that are provided to those who cannot make ends meet in specific circumstances.

Each of these types of social security will factor into your estate plan. Here is a look at how each of them can work for you.

Social security retirement payments

Social security retirement payments are paid out once you hit your retirement age, based on how much income you have earned over the course of your lifetime. Anyone who has worked in the United States and has paid into the system can begin to collect retirement payments as early as age 62. But full retirement ages depend on when you were born. The federal government is extending this from age 65 (for those born before 1943) to 66 (for those born between 1943 and 1959) to 67 (for those born after 1959.) Social security retirement payments also are dependent on how much you have earned. Depending on that information, for 2009, you can receive as little as $1,000 per month, or up to $2,323 per month. These numbers are adjusted per person.

To understand how this type of social security factors into your retirement plan, you first need to take into account the way that it helps you have the funds that you need for your retirement years. For many, it can provide enough funds, coupled with other funds from pensions and your estate, to help you live a decent retirement. Yet it also should be factored into your estate plan. It should function as money for you to spend during your retirement years that will supplement the other income that you bring in from your estate.

For most people, this gives two options. They can use their social security income to increase the amount of money they have available to them on a monthly basis and simply spend more during that time, or they can leave more of their assets in their estate plan untouched and use social security for their expenses.

The latter option would leave more for your heirs in the long run, but you should be aware that social security payments can play a role in the cost of your estate tax, should there be too much left over when you die.

You can learn exactly when and how much you can draw on your social security by calling the Social Security Administration (800-772-1213) or visiting their Web site (**www.ssa.gov**). You can also find your local office by visiting their site.

Disability benefits

Some individuals are eligible for disability benefits from social security if they are injured and no longer can earn an income. This book has revealed how disability insurance works in the Chapter 10, and this type of disability benefit is somewhat the same. The amount of money that you can get through this program depends on how much you have earned and saved into social security.

Disability is not likely to make you rich, as it provides only a modest amount of money that is designed to help you to pay for your expenses while you cannot work. For those who are injured, this type of protection can help save them from having to sell their home to pay for their expenses. If you carry disability until you reach your full retirement age, they simply convert from "disability" into "retirement" payments, although the amount does not change. You can find out how much you would get if you were injured today through the Social Security Administration.

One important note for estate planning reasons: It is recommended that you do not rely solely on the disability benefits that you can obtain. It is unlikely that these benefits would be enough to pay all your expenses, especially if you are injured younger and have had less time to put money into social security. It is highly recommended that you go back and read the information we have provided in Chapter 10 about disability insurance, which is something that can help you make all ends meet.

Finally, disability benefits will not affect much of your estate plan, as the funds are likely to be relatively low.

Survivor benefits

Survivor benefits are a portion of funds that come from your social security investments. If you die and leave behind a spouse or children, they are likely to be provided with survivor benefits. Sometimes, even divorced spouses will qualify for these benefits.

The amount of money that can be obtained through survivor benefits again depends on how much you have put into social security, which you can learn by contacting the Social Security Administration. It is likely that this amount will not provide enough funds to maintain your family's current lifestyle. For most, it does not provide enough help to your family because it is not the same amount as your paycheck.

For this reason, we recommend revisiting Chapter 10 and considering the value of adding life insurance to your estate plan, as this can provide enough funds for your family to maintain the quality of life they are accustomed to and help them avoid losing your home or other assets.

As for your estate plan, determine what your survivor benefits are. Then, figure out how that fits into your need for additional life insurance, as well as other benefits that your family will have when you die. In some cases, it will be enough to keep you from needing to purchase a higher life insurance policy. Work with your insurance provider to help you make ends meet.

Supplemental security income

Supplement security income (SSI) is another form of social security, but it is not something you should rely on. Only those who are needy, such as those who have little property or are disabled, will be able to take advantage of this benefit.

The only way that this type of benefit plays into an estate plan is as a last resort. If you have lost most of your estate, these benefits may be able to kick in and provide you with the funds that you need. They tend to be unfortunate and tragic events that put you in this position, and not something that you plan for.

401(k) and similar retirement plans

Many companies that do not offer pension plans will provide 401(k) plans as their way of helping employees save for their retirement years. They are somewhat like IRA accounts, but a bit different. They tend to have a few restrictions on them, and there are different limits.

A 401(k) tends to be from a company that is privately held or publicly traded; 403b and 457 plans are different, as they are for government workers and others who work in tax-exempt organizations. You will need to know exactly what type of plan you have so that you can learn its effect on your estate.

Many companies will match the contributions that you make into your 401(k), while others will put in a smaller percentage. Most companies provide from 10 to 20 percent of what you put into your 401(k). You also need to learn how "vested" you are. Some companies limit the funds that can be taken with you if you leave the company (based solely on the amount that the company has matched) to an amount that is called your vested value. The higher this value, the more the funds that have been matched by your employer factor into your funds.

As implied, a 401(k) is an investment tool that can be taken with you when you leave your employer. You will have a certain amount of time to move those funds into another tax advantages account without having to face penalties on the funds.

When you open a 401(k), you will need to name your beneficiaries. If you are married at that time, this must be your spouse. The spouse can waive these funds if they decide it is in their best interest. If you die before your spouse, your spouse will choose whether they need to withdraw the funds from your 401(k) in a lump sum or through payments. Indeed, you will need to determine how much income tax they will be charged in these cases. With that said, you should also know that your 401(k) proceeds, when passed to your beneficiary, do not go through probate.

If you have a 401(k), it is important that you work out several key matters with your financial planner:

- Determine how much you have in your 401(k) and how it is being invested.

- Determine what advantages you have to this type of plan over others, as well as the disadvantages of having it.

- Determine how much you can invest in your 401(k) for the maximum benefit without running into taxation problems.

- Determine the best payment plan option for you and your family when you begin to draw on those funds during your retirement years.

- Revisit and adjust your 401(k) balances and investments as necessary throughout your life to adjust for risk tolerance.

IRA accounts

Somewhat more common than the 401(k) are IRA accounts. IRAs are different plans, though. The laws regarding them are often changed, which is one of the most important reasons why you need to work with a financial planner to assess your situation with them. IRAs are tax-deductible contributions under special amounts. For example, Congress determines how much you can put into your IRA each year. For the year 2009, you were able to contribute $5,000 to your traditional and Roth IRA. For those who are 50 or older, you can put more into your account — termed catch-up contributions. It is important to work with your financial planner in regard to your IRA. You need to ensure that you do not invest against your goals for the long-term.

As with any investment, you put money away into an IRA each year. When you retire, the funds are used to pay for your retirement, or you can leave them there as part of your estate. How you plan to use your IRA should help you decide how much you need to have tucked away.

You also need to name your beneficiary for the IRA, who will receive the funds from your account when you die. Your IRA funds will not go through probate at this time, but your beneficiaries will need to pay taxes on the funds that are given to them. Indeed, you will also need to pay taxes on these dollars when you use them. A Roth IRA is a similar situation, but here you invest dollars after taxing, which would mean that you do not pay them when you withdraw those funds.

Just as you deliberated these areas for your 401(k), it is important to take them into consideration with an IRA:

- Determine how much you have in your IRA and how it is being invested.

- Determine what advantages you have to this type of plan over others, as well as the disadvantages of having it.
- Determine how much you can invest in your IRA for the maximum benefit without running into taxation problems.
- Determine the best payment plan option for you and your family when you begin to draw on those funds during your retirement years.
- Revisit and adjust your IRA balances and investments as necessary throughout your life to adjust for risk tolerance.

It is also important for you to look into the various types of IRAs out there. There are many, each with its own benefits. With the help of your financial planner, you will be able to determine what the right type of IRA is for you. You should compare them, as some have better tax advantages than others.

All these retirement accounts and plans allow you to invest in your future. As we have mentioned, it is important for you to think about how you will use those funds, though. For some, the goal is to provide the funds as a way of funding the living expenses, travel, and medical expenses they will incur during retirement years. For others, they are funds tucked away to be placed as part of their estate to leave behind to heirs. In any of these situations, realize that your use of the funds is completely up to you. Plan your estate with your options in mind.

Water Mill Along The Blue Ridge Parkway, Virginia

Chapter 13

What Happens When...?

Life is not simple, neat, or easily organized, even with the best-laid plans. There are always situations that you cannot plan for because you do not know what could potentially happen. Yet, the unique aspect of estate planning is that you can plan for the possibility of many things that could possibly occur. This chapter will address some of the unique situations that often cause people's estates to get out of line.

Children and Estates

We have touched upon the topic of children in earlier chapters, but here are some details to ensure your children will be taken care of. The first consideration is to define what is meant by "children." Different rules need to be considered for adult children and for minors (under the age of 18). In each of these situations, different needs must be met.

For minor children, there are two main concerns to consider:

1. Who will take care of your children if you die before they reach 18?

2. How can you provide financial stability to your children if you die before they reach 18? This includes everyday living expenses, as well as schooling.

Who will take care of your children if you die before they are adults?

To answer that question, understand that, if there is a second parent (one survives the other), this parent will most likely have custody of the child. When there is no other parent available, a personal guardian must be established for the child. In estate planning, this process is separate from naming godparents. To document and make official who this person should be, you will need to include it in your will. This is one reason why you need a will at all stages of your life. Yet, this person will not become your children's guardian until the court system has deemed it after you die. If for some reason a judge believes that the child should not be with the person you name, the court has the ability and discretion to change this person. This tends to only happen when someone contests your will's naming, and even then is rare, unless they can prove that this person simply should not be caring for children.

When choosing someone to care for your children, you must take into consideration their willingness and ability. Do not assume they will do it, as this is something that should be thoroughly thought-out. You should also have a secondary person listed in case the first one is unable to take on your children for some reason. In addition, you should name one sole person as their guardian rather than a couple. There are potential problems with naming a couple, including who will get the children if that couple splits up.

You can name a guardian for each of your children, or one for all them. If you feel that it is necessary to break up your children in order to provide them with the type of relationship that is most fruitful, that is exactly what you can do in your will.

Note that just choosing a guardian is not enough to completely fill in the blanks for that child. What is more, it does not give anyone the right to manage the funds that should be given to this child. We will talk about the financial aspect shortly.

Unfortunately, we cannot provide you with any specific answers about what to do if you do not want the other parent of your child to get guardianship if something happens to you. Each case has to be handled on a per-case basis. First, you should name whomever you do want to raise them in your will. Second, if the case is not contested by someone, that person is whom the judge is likely to appoint as your child's guardian. If the case is contested, the only way for the judge to not provide the surviving parent with custody of the child is to determine that the parent is unfit to raise the child based on legitimate information, or that the parent has abandoned the child.

The only action for you to take is to use a letter as part of your will that defines what your concerns are and why you have chosen one person over another. You can explain these decisions in the content of your will as well.

How can you provide financial stability to your children if you die before they reach 18?

The next question that you have to answer is who will manage your child's property until they are old enough to do so. Minors can only own between $2,500 and $5,000 themselves without adult control. This means that you need to appoint someone to manage your child's money. This person will then be called a "trustee," "custodian," or "property guardian." You can also assign someone who will manage your children's property until they reach a specific age, say 21, 25, or even 35.

As we have mentioned throughout this book, there are a variety of ways that you can set up these funds. You can use any of these four methods to leave property behind for your minor child:

1. Custodianship, which works under the Uniform Transfers to Minor Act
2. A trust for the child
3. A family pot trust
4. A property guardianship

Uniform Transfers to Minors Act

In all states except for South Carolina and Vermont, you can leave property to your children under this law. The person placed in charge of the funds is called the "custodian," and their management of the property in Virginia ends when the child reaches 18, the age of majority. The only exception to this would be if a will or a trust dictated that the child has to achieve a later age, in which case the terms of the controlling document will prevail.

In this law, you will document, either through your will or through your living will, what property should be given to your minor child. You name the person who will act as custodian as well as a successor, in cases where the first custodian cannot perform his duties. You finally note that you want the property managed "under the state's Uniform Transfers to Minors Act." This gives this person the ability to collect, hold, invest, reinvest, and manage the property as they see fit. He or she must keep detailed records for tax records to be filed but does not need to file a separate return. The custodian is allowed a reasonable compensation for managing these funds unless it is waived. Virginia also requires a guardian to provide a bond to insure the integrity of the child's funds will be preserved during the term of the guardianship, and guardians are accountable to the courts for their actions as guardians.. Virginia Code section 31-14 states in this regard:

"The circuit courts may hear and determine all matters between guardians and their wards, require settlements of guardianship accounts, remove any guardian for neglect or breach of trust, and appoint another in his stead, and make any order for the custody, health, maintenance, education and support of an infant and the management, disbursement, preservation, and investment of his estate."

Trusts for children

There are two types of trusts that can be set up to manage your child's funds: a child's trust or a family pot trust. The difference is that in a child's trust, you leave specific property to a specific child, whereas with a family pot trust, all the property is left to all children and can then be used in any amount by each of the children.

With any trust, a person is placed in charge of the property. The documents that establish the trust define what the trustee's responsibilities and rights are. You can establish this trust with a living trust or with a will. A benefit to using a living trust to do this is you forgo any probate costs that could be used otherwise.

The property in the trust is managed by the trustee until the beneficiaries, — in this case, your children — reach the age at which you have deemed that they will get what is in the trust. You can name this age yourself, but you should consider why you need it to last for such a long time, such as beyond the age of 30 to 35. If the child will not be able to mentally handle the property, it is also possible to set up a special-needs trust to care for them with these funds without giving them control of them. In most cases, the property is managed by the trustee for uses in education, medical necessities, and living expenses.

Determine what your ultimate goals are. When children are younger, a family pot trust can be better used to serve the children's needs as a whole. When children are older, or when there is a large gap in their ages, a child's trust can allow for the property to be more evenly distributed to each of the children.

Property guardian

Using a property guardian is rare and is not typically a wise decision. For example, when you leave property to your children to be managed by a property guardian, the property must go through probate, which means taxes. In addition, property guardians are often required to report for court reviews and face strict, limiting abilities on how they can use the funds. You also have no ability to extend the property guardian's abilities beyond the age of 18. Indeed, it is costly with the fees for attorneys and does nothing to provide you with any idea that the property guardian will do a good job with the children's property.

If you will be using this type of arrangement, it will work for those who have minor children that will be earning a substantial amount of money after you die or if they will receive a large gift or inheritance that does not name its own property manager. There are other situations in which it can be beneficial, but you must carefully consider these.

Compare the various ways in which you can leave property to your child after you die. Work with your financial planning attorney to figure out which method provides the best outcome for your situation.

Your child's education

Saving for your child's education is an important consideration for anyone, and it should be part of your estate plan. Tax saving education investment plans are offered in two different types: 529 plans and Coverdell accounts. Each should be carefully considered for its benefits and disadvantages.

529 plans

A 529 plan is a tax-free investment that you can make to pay for higher education expenses to the person that you name as the beneficiary. This person has to be a family member, and this plan does allow for you to include this type of fund for any of your children or other young family relations. Because you can contribute to the 529 plan without having to pay taxes, and no income tax is assessed on the money that ends up coming from this fund, it is an ideal tax situation to be in. The funds must be used for qualified expenses, which are tuition, books, fees, supplies, and other aspects for college, graduate school, or other institutions.

You can contribute up to $12,000 per year to each of these plans. A couple can give up to $24,000 per year. Anything over this, and you will be facing a federal gift tax penalty. If you contribute up to $60,000 in one year and do not make future contributions for the next five years, this can help you to avoid the penalty, but you must live this long as well. If funds are withdrawn for any other purpose, the funds are subject to taxes.

These plans are based on state law rather than on federal law, and therefore, you can only use them if the plan is state-authorized. Every state has some type of 529 plan for you to take advantage of. Management companies are in place to manage these based on whom the state has chosen to do so. In many states, anyone can contribute to these funds for the beneficiary, allowing grandparents, aunts, and uncles to do so. For example, Virginia's 529 plan allows for parents and grandparents to contribute to an education.

You should understand that these plans are securities of various types, including stocks and bonds. Some states have far more aggressive plans than others. You need to select the right 529 plan for your situation. Virginia offers four types of investment plans. Beginning in 2009, Virginia allowed an annual 529 deduction of up to $4,000. Your financial planning team can help you consider this need.

There are some factors that could be potential drawbacks of a 529 plan. There are often highly expensive fees for these plans for the management companies. This can be higher than 2 percent annually. You should understand what these fees are before you agree to the plan. Also, look into the disclosure policies that the company uses so that you can find out what is going on with your money.

Take the time to learn what types of plans are available to you and what stipulations are in place regarding them. Each state has a different 529 plan, making it hard for you to learn what the plan offers unless you talk to your financial planner. The other drawback of these plans is that they offer limited investment tools. It is often necessary for you to determine whether you are all right with having just a handful of securities to invest in or whether you want a broader range of investment opportunities. Of course, no matter which plan you select, there is no guarantee that they will deliver any investment benefit to you.

Virginia's Web site for finding more information on 529 plans is **www.virginia529.com**.

Coverdell accounts

Once called educational IRAs, these accounts allow you to contribute up to $2,000 per year per person investing in a beneficiary's account. These contributions are not tax-deductible at the time they are made, but the account is not taxed when it grows, and there is no tax assessed when the withdrawals (for qualified expenses) are taken.

The benefit with this type of educational investment tool is that you get a larger range of investment choices, which means you are able to personally manage the investments more so than with a 529 plan.

The largest drawback is the limited amount that can be contributed per year to these funds, but they work well for those with young children. Grandparents or others can also invest in these as an additional investment.

These educational and other methods of taking care of your child, when you cannot literally do so, are important to consider as part of your estate. Are there other concerns that you have, such as caring for children that are not biologically yours? Perhaps you would like to disinherit a child? These things also can be worked into your estate plan, but with the help of your attorney per specific situation. Handling these on a per-case basis is important.

What Happens with Divorce?

Another situation that is often tricky to plan for is divorce. If you are going through a divorce, or do in the future, it is important to think about your estate plan in the process. It is not something that is planned for, but if it happens, you need to consider how it will affect your estate plan. There are several key items that need to be taken into consideration, including what will happen to your property and children if you do nothing, and what options you have.

In situations like these, you need a specialized attorney, one who has experience in divorce and in estate planning, as the two can be rather tricky to plan.

There is more to settling a divorce than just looking at the property you have in the here and now; you also need to factor in the property in your estate and its future there. You both have an estate plan for what will happen when you die, which may include a number of different people from both sides of the family. Yet when you do divorce, you might not want to have these people in the same situations. In most cases, your estate is split 50/50 during a divorce, which means that the property in your estate has changed from being fully yours to now being half yours.

Although to this point, you are likely considering your estate as "our property," it is important to define it as "my property and your property." During your marriage, you both likely made purchases that were solely in one person's name. Yet during a divorce, all property that is purchased during the marriage falls under "marital property." The bottom line is that you need to inventory what comes to you after the divorce and reassess your estate plan now that it has changed.

Complete the following steps to reassess your estate plan:

- Overhaul your estate and gift tax marital deductions.
- Redo your will to include a more accurate picture of your life.
- Determine who should get property when you die, including property that you left to your ex-spouse.
- Determine your child's situation in regard to the estate now, which should also include stepchildren, if applicable.

You can still leave property to your spouse, if you decide to do that.

The best course of action during a divorce, and afterward, is to determine what property you still have and to arrange your estate plan accordingly. Children can be provided for just as you would before, depending on one or both of your new estate plans. Work closely with your attorney to make these changes in your estate plan as soon as possible after the divorce.

Chapter 14

Putting It All Together

Putting together your estate plan can seem like a huge task, one that involves various elements and can, in short, easily overwhelm someone from the start. Yet that is why we have explained the importance of hiring several key people to help you through the process. The first thing you need to do is look at your estate planning team, making sure that they have the skill and the experience — and that you can trust them.

At this point, you should have a basic understanding of what goes into an estate plan and what you would like to include in yours. Ideally, we have opened your eyes to a few situations in which you can easily craft your wishes and even avoid costly taxes in the process. Let us organize those thoughts here to get you started in the actual planning of your estate.

Step 1: Why Are You Planning?

The biggest reason to put together a comprehensive estate plan is as simple as being able to control what happens to your property after you die. But even if you do not care what happens to it — which is not the case most of the time — you still need to consider what will happen to your heirs if you do not plan anything.

Chances are high that they will contribute to the tax system with some high costs on probate and estate taxes coming from your property. If you have any real property that is valuable, there might be a fight, a family problem, or even the loss of that property in an effort to choose where it goes. In the end, an estate can rip a family apart with the "I should get this" and "You do not deserve anything" problems that many families deal with.

You might have your own reason for planning your estate. Perhaps you want to make sure someone does not get something, or you want specific pieces of your estate to go to a certain person. You may just want to make sure that the government does not get too much of your property in the taxes that end up being paid from it.

The point is that you should define why you want to plan your estate so that you can make sure that in the end, your estate plan reflects this desire.

Step 2: What Do I Want to Cover?

Every person's life is unique, and with that comes a variety of struggles with what happens in the estate that they plan. Nevertheless, you need to sit down and ask yourself what you need to do in your estate plan. Set forth a few goals that can help to dictate what happens. For many people, this means determining where large assets go and who gets what. The best way to do this is to simply look at the situation from all points of view.

For example, if you have two children and want them each to get a fair share in your estate, how will you make that happen? Perhaps you could have the family home sold and each will get a share of it. But if you know that your daughter would love to keep the family home in the family, perhaps a life insurance policy for the value of the home could be made up to fund the same dollar value to your son. Look at all options available to you in planning your estate.

If your goal is to minimize the amount of taxes that go to the government when you die, there are likely to be plenty of ways to do this, if you work on it before you die. As you read in our estate tax section, there is little doubt that you can minimize this number, but often, much of this has to be done ahead of time.

The question then to ask is, what do you want your estate plan to encompass?

Step 3: Who Are Your Beneficiaries?

Defining who will benefit from your estate plan is an important and often worrisome situation. While you might love to leave something to each of your family members, it is likely that you want to make sure that certain people are taken care of in your estate plan. Of course, you also need to think of yourself in the process. How will you plan for your retirement years?

Consider the people whom you want to take care of in your will:

- How will you care for your spouse?
- How will you care for your children?
- Are there stepchildren, adopted children, or other family members whom you want to care for?
- Do you plan to leave most of your property for your children, or perhaps your grandchildren?
- Are there charities that you want to support?

- How will you care for yourself during your retirement years?
- What type of allotment do you need to make for health care, including long-term care and expensive medical treatments for worst-case scenarios?
- Are there others you want to take care of through your will? If so, how will you do that?

It is important to consider the importance of each of these people. For example, while your second cousin may be someone you want to leave something to, you want to make sure that your children have the funds necessary for their college education first. Take the time to list those you want to include in your will by importance and the needs that each one has.

Step 4: Caring for Your Children

Although we touched on it in the previous step, often it takes time to consider what needs to be done to care for children. Depending on when you are crafting your estate plan, you might have minor children to plan for. In that case, you need to be concerned with such things as your child's custody, your child's property that you plan to leave them, and the educational needs of that child. Even if you do not die while your child is a minor, you want to plan for their college education, and your estate should be how you do that.

There are many methods that can help you accomplish these goals. We have talked about the process of selecting guardianship, how to establish trusts for your child, and even how to establish educational products to protect their college education.

Yet minor children are not the only ones who should be taken care of. You will want to address the needs of adult children, too, and how you will provide for them when you are no longer able to be there.

Step 5: Determine Where You Are Currently

With an understanding of what you want to accomplish in your estate plan, the next step involves simply figuring out where you stand right now. You should first start by determining your estate's value. You also want to consider what you need to accomplish your goals. While everyone wants to leave behind millions of dollars, be sensible in developing a plan that provides for what you realistically can accomplish in your lifetime.

There are two items to consider here:

1. What do you currently own that should be included in your estate?
2. What do you want to earn or add to your value in order to accomplish your estate planning goals?

The person to help you answer question No. 2 is your financial planner, who can help you determine how you will accomplish all your financial goals throughout your lifetime so that when you die, your estate plan is where you want it to be.

As you plan your estate, you should first plan for what you currently have so that ultimately, your estate plan only includes what you have, not what you expect to have. But as life progresses, you will need to go back and make changes as necessary.

Step 6: Who Is Your Team?

In the first chapters of this book, we talked about the wide range of people that were on your estate planning team. Now is the time to assemble them and to develop a plan with each one of them. Your estate planning attorney, your financial planner, your accountant, and your insurance agent are valuable to you during this time. But do not make the mistake of thinking that anyone can play these roles.

You need to make sure that:

- Your team has experience in estate planning. They must be competent in this particular field to serve you.
- Your team has proven success and plenty of references for you to check out.
- Your team consists of people (not companies necessarily, but real people) you trust wholeheartedly with your financial future and your heirs' property.

Spending some time finding people who can help you with these goals is important. You need an insurance agent, for example, who will tell you how much insurance you need, not how much they can convince you that you need. You need a financial planner who is not working for the investments that they are pushing. You want to know that they have your interests in mind throughout this process.

Once you have assembled your team, take the information that you have gathered from steps 1 through 5 and talk to them about it. Ask them to help you develop plans to make your goals come to life. Going in educated gives you the advantage here.

Step 7: Whom Should You Tell?

Even if you have an estate plan in place, you should still make an effort to provide your family with all the information and plans you are making. How many times have you heard stories of families that are torn apart because one child got more than the other in their parent's estate? Even worse, many do not understand what is left over and the value of those aspects to the parent. You might place a high value on a simple charm that you are passing down to your grandchild, but the one who gets the car might seem to have gotten more.

The point is that you need to make sure everyone in your estate plan — and even those you have intentionally left out — knows what to expect. Of course, you do not have to do this. You can die being the only one who even knows that the estate plan is in effect — although, ideally, at least your spouse knows.

In addition to these people, you will want to make sure that your trusted friends and family know that you do have an estate plan so that they can help to make sure it comes to life in the event that your will cannot be found.

As you make changes to your estate plan, make sure that you update those that you have included in your estate plan. Otherwise, this can cause a number of problems later.

Step 8: Did You Get Everything?

It is important to review several details as you develop them. As you create your estate plan, it can become easy for you to forget certain situations and even find yourself struggling with the specifics of each.

Here are a few commonly forgotten areas that you do not want to forget:

- Include a residuary clause, which will provide for whatever is left over in your estate. Anything that you do not specifically mention in your will should have a destination to go to so that there is no problem.

- Include contingent beneficiaries in your will who will take over for those who cannot inherit what you provide. For example, if someone you list as a beneficiary dies before you do and you do not change your will, the contingent beneficiary gets whatever the beneficiary would have.

- Is your personal representative still someone you trust to handle your situation? As your life changes, this person may change, too. Look at all situations where you list beneficiaries and guardians to determine whether changes should be made there.

- Make sure that your will is properly legalized, as well as any trusts, insurance policies, or other estate plans. Notaries are the best witnesses, as they do not have anything to do with you and therefore are not in any way benefiting from what you are signing.

- Do not rush it. Estate planning does take time, and you do need to plan your will and estate based on a lifetime, in many cases. Take the time to go through all aspects of your will so that you can make sure that ultimately, the best plans are laid for your future and your property after you die.

Working with skilled professionals in developing your estate plan should minimize the problems that you face, of course. Nevertheless, no one, no matter how much they can be trusted, is behind your goals as much as you are. Therefore, do your own checking to make sure that your will and estate plan are what you want them to be.

Step 9: Revisit Your Estate Plan Yearly or More

Even once you have your estate plan in order, you still need to go back to it and look at it a bit closer each year. Life changes, and it does so often. You should even try to have your attorney book a time slot for you each year about the same time — say around your birthday — to come in and find out whether anything in your estate plan needs to be readjusted. As your property grows in value, it might be necessary to reassess its effect on the estate plan.

Also, any time that you make serious changes to your estate, such as purchasing real estate, selling real estate, or making other significant changes, revisit your estate plan to make changes as necessary. If you sell a home that was supposed to go to your daughter because you needed the funds to support your retirement years, you first need to remove it from your estate plan. You may also want to return to the estate plan and readjust it to now give your daughter a share of the other home that you own, so that she and her brother get an even share.

As part of revisiting your will, it will become important to consider the facts and how they relate to your estate tax situation, too. You might find yourself just over the estate tax threshold and therefore needing to make adjustments to minimize that level of estate taxable property.

Step 10: Work to Accomplish Your Goals

Even after you have succeeded in developing your estate plan, you will have to work on it to accomplish your goals. The good news is that there are plenty of ways for you to put together an estate plan that is effective in what it does based on what you currently have. But for those who need to add more value to their estate, you need to do just that.

It is important to consider the importance of your estate plan in relation to your life, too. Life changes, and you might simply change your mind about certain details. When that happens, make alterations to your estate plan to reflect this.

Conclusion

There is no doubt that you will need the help of a skilled team of professionals to help you accomplish the goals that you have in regard to your estate plan. Virtually anything that you want to achieve in your will and estate plan can be done, but it is important to remain vigilant and see it through.

Work through this book to see what options you have for overcoming the various obstacles that often get in the way while planning an estate. Indeed, if you learned anything, it should be that it is essential to plan your estate in some form, so that when you are no longer around to make decisions, what you want to have happen, happens.

By carefully planning your estate, you can accomplish all your goals, from leaving property for your heirs to caring for your minor children, and even making sure that your favorite charities are taken care of. Even if you just want to make sure that your estate pays as little tax as it can, that in itself is a reason to plan your estate.

No one wants to think about death, but you need to consider what will happen to your life's work after you are no longer here — or risk it all.

Shenandoah National Park, Luray, Virginia

Appendix A

VIRGINIA ADVANCE MEDICAL DIRECTIVE

(Statutory Form, IC 15-35-4-10)

Author's Note: *An advance directive executed pursuant to this article may, but need not, be in the following form. Note there are various options to consider in selection.*

I, ____________, willfully and voluntarily make known my wishes in the event that I am incapable of making an informed decision, as follows: I understand that my advance directive may include the selection of an agent, as well as set forth my choices regarding health care. The term "health care" means the furnishing of services to any individual for the purpose of preventing, alleviating, curing, or healing human illness, injury, or physical disability, including, but not limited to, medications; surgery; blood transfusions; chemotherapy; radiation therapy; admission to a hospital, assisted living facility, or other health care facility; psychiatric or other mental health treatment; and life-prolonging procedures and palliative care.

The phrase "incapable of making an informed decision" means unable to understand the nature, extent, and probable consequences of a proposed health care decision, or unable to make a rational evaluation of the risks and benefits of a proposed health care decision as compared with the risks and benefits of alternatives to that decision, or unable to communicate such understanding in any way. The determination that I am incapable of making an informed decision shall be made by my attending physician and a second physician or licensed clinical psychologist after a personal examination of me, and shall be certified in writing. The second physician or licensed clinical psychologist shall not be otherwise currently involved in my treatment, unless such independent physician or licensed clinical psychologist is not reasonably available. Such certification shall be required before health care is provided, continued, withheld, or withdrawn, before any named agent shall be granted authority to make health care decisions on my behalf; and before, or as soon as reasonably practicable after, health care is provided, continued, withheld, or withdrawn, and every 180 days thereafter while the need for health care continues.

If, at any time, I am determined to be incapable of making an informed decision, I shall be notified, to the extent I am capable of receiving such notice, that such determination has been made before health care is provided, continued, withheld, or withdrawn. Such notice shall also be provided, as soon as practical, to my named agent or person authorized by § 54.1-2986 to make health care decisions on my behalf. If I am later determined to be capable of making an informed decision by a physician, in writing, upon personal examination, any further health care decisions will require my informed consent.

(SELECT ANY OR ALL OF THE OPTIONS BELOW.)

OPTION I: APPOINTMENT OF AGENT (CROSS THROUGH OPTIONS I AND II BELOW IF YOU DO NOT WANT TO APPOINT AN AGENT TO MAKE HEALTH CARE DECISIONS FOR YOU.)

I hereby appoint ______________ *(primary agent)*, of ______________ *(address and telephone number)*, as my agent to make health care decisions on my behalf as authorized in this document.

If ______________ *(primary agent)* is not reasonably available or is unable or unwilling to act as my agent, then I appoint ______________ *(successor agent)*, of ______________ *(address and telephone number)*, to serve in that capacity.

I hereby grant to my agent, named above, full power and authority to make health care decisions on my behalf as described below whenever I have been determined to be incapable of making an informed decision. My agent's authority hereunder is effective as long as I am incapable of making an informed decision.

In exercising the power to make health care decisions on my behalf, my agent shall follow my desires and preferences as stated in this document or as otherwise known to my agent. My agent shall be guided by my medical diagnosis and prognosis and any information provided by my physicians as to the intrusiveness, pain, risks, and side effects associated with treatment or nontreatment. My agent shall not make any decision regarding my health care that he knows, or upon reasonable inquiry ought to know, is contrary to my religious beliefs or my basic values, whether expressed orally or in writing. If my agent cannot determine what health care choice I would have made on my own behalf, then my agent shall make a choice for me based upon what he believes to be in my best interests.

OPTION II: POWERS OF MY AGENT (CROSS THROUGH ANY LANGUAGE YOU DO NOT WANT AND ADD ANY LANGUAGE YOU DO WANT.)

The powers of my agent shall include the following:

A. To consent to or refuse or withdraw consent to any type of health care, treatment, surgical procedure, diagnostic procedure, medication and the use of mechanical or other procedures that affect any bodily function, including, but not limited to, artificial respiration, artificially administered nutrition and hydration, and cardiopulmonary resuscitation. This authorization specifically includes the power to consent to the administration of dosages of pain-relieving medication in excess of recommended dosages in an amount sufficient to relieve pain, even if such medication carries the risk of addiction or of inadvertently hastening my death;

B. To request, receive, and review any information, verbal or written, regarding my physical or mental health, including, but not limited to, medical and hospital records, and to consent to the disclosure of this information;

C. To employ and discharge my health care providers;

D. To authorize my admission to or discharge (including transfer to another facility) from any hospital, hospice, nursing home, assisted living facility, or other medical care facility. If I have authorized admission to a health care facility for treatment of mental illness, that authority is stated elsewhere in this advance directive.

E. To authorize my admission to a health care facility for the treatment of mental illness for no more than 10 calendar days, provided I do not protest the admission; and a physician on the staff of or designated by the proposed admitting facility examines me and states in writing that I have a mental illness and I am incapable of making an informed decision about my admission, and that I need treatment in the facility; and to authorize my discharge (including transfer to another facility) from the facility;

F. To authorize my admission to a health care facility for the treatment of mental illness for no more than 10 calendar days, even over my protest, if a physician on the staff of or designated by the proposed admitting facility examines me and states in writing that I have a mental illness and I am incapable of making an informed decision about my admission, and that I need treatment in the facility; and to authorize my discharge (including transfer to another facility) from the facility. My physician or licensed clinical psychologist hereby attests that I am capable of making an informed decision and that I understand the consequences of this provision of my advance directive: ______________________________];

G. To authorize the specific types of health care identified in this advance directive [specify cross-reference to other sections of directive], even over my protest. My physician or licensed clinical psychologist hereby attests that I am capable of making an informed decision and that I understand the consequences of this provision of my advance directive: ______________________________];

H. To continue to serve as my agent even in the event that I protest the agent's authority after I have been determined to be incapable of making an informed decision;

I. To authorize my participation in any health care study approved by an institutional review board or research review committee according to applicable federal or state law that offers the prospect of direct therapeutic benefit to me;

J. To authorize my participation in any health care study approved by an institutional review board or research review committee pursuant to applicable federal or state law that aims to increase scientific understanding of any condition that I may have or otherwise to promote human well-being, even though it offers no prospect of direct benefit to me;

K. To make decisions regarding visitation during any time that I am admitted to any health care facility, consistent with the following directions: ______________________________; and

L. To take any lawful actions that may be necessary to carry out these decisions, including the granting of releases of liability to medical providers.

Further, my agent shall not be liable for the costs of health care pursuant to his or her authorization, based solely on that authorization.

OPTION III: HEALTH CARE INSTRUCTIONS (CROSS THROUGH PARAGRAPHS A AND/OR B IF YOU DO NOT WANT TO GIVE ADDITIONAL SPECIFIC INSTRUCTIONS ABOUT YOUR HEALTH CARE.)

A. I specifically direct that I receive the following health care if it is medically appropriate under the circumstances as determined by my attending physician: ______________________________

B. I specifically direct that the following health care not be provided to me under the following circumstances (you may specify that certain health care not be provided under any circumstances): __________

____

OPTION IV: END-OF-LIFE INSTRUCTIONS (CROSS THROUGH THIS OPTION IF YOU DO NOT WANT TO GIVE INSTRUCTIONS ABOUT YOUR HEALTH CARE IF YOU HAVE A TERMINAL CONDITION.)

If at any time my attending physician should determine that I have a terminal condition where the application of life-prolonging procedures — including artificial respiration, cardiopulmonary resuscitation, artificially administered nutrition, and artificially administered hydration — would serve only to artificially prolong the dying process, I direct that such procedures be withheld or withdrawn, and that I be permitted to die naturally with only the administration of medication or the performance of any medical procedure deemed necessary to provide me with comfort care or to alleviate pain.

OPTION: OTHER DIRECTIONS ABOUT LIFE-PROLONGING PROCEDURES. (If you wish to provide your own directions, or if you wish to add to the directions you have given above, you may do so here. If you wish to give specific instructions regarding certain life-prolonging procedures, such as artificial respiration, cardiopulmonary resuscitation, artificially administered nutrition, and artificially administered hydration, this is where you should write them.) I direct that: __________________

____

____

____

____

OPTION: My other instructions regarding my care if I have a terminal condition are as follows: ________________________________

____

____

____

In the absence of my ability to give directions regarding the use of such life-prolonging procedures, it is my intention that this advance directive shall be honored by my family and physician as the final expression of my legal right to refuse health care and acceptance of the consequences of such refusal.

OPTION V: APPOINTMENT OF AN AGENT TO MAKE AN ANATOMICAL GIFT OR ORGAN, TISSUE, OR EYE DONATION (CROSS THROUGH IF YOU DO NOT WANT TO APPOINT AN AGENT TO MAKE AN ANATOMICAL GIFT OR ANY ORGAN, TISSUE, OR EYE DONATION FOR YOU.)

Upon my death, I direct that an anatomical gift of all of my body or certain organ, tissue or eye donations may be made pursuant to Article 2 (§ 32.1-289.2 et seq.) of Chapter 8 of Title 32.1 and in accordance with my directions, if any.

I hereby appoint ________________ as my agent, of ______________ *(address and telephone number)*, to make any such anatomical gift or organ, tissue, or eye donation following my death. I further direct that: _______ ____ *(declarant's directions concerning anatomical gift or organ, tissue, or eye donation)*.

This advance directive shall not terminate in the event of my disability.

AFFIRMATION AND RIGHT TO REVOKE:

By signing below, I indicate that I am emotionally and mentally capable of making this advance directive and that I understand the purpose and effect of this document. I understand I may revoke all or any part of this document at any time:

(i) with a signed, dated writing;

(ii) by physical cancellation or destruction of this advance directive by myself, or by directing someone else to destroy it in my presence; or

(iii) by my oral expression of intent to revoke.

____________________ ______________________________________

(Date) *(Signature of Declarant)*

The declarant signed the foregoing advance directive in my presence.

(Witness) ____

(Witness) ____

Air Force Memorial, Arlington, Virginia

Appendix B

The following pages provide you with samples of various wills and legal papers involved in planning your estate. Because state laws vary, be sure to consult with your attorney before relying solely on the examples.

Living Will

This declaration was made this ______day of _____________, 20____.

I, ______________________________, of my own volition, hereby make known my wish that my life not be prolonged by the use of any machines under the circumstances, which I have included below.

If I become terminally ill, and my doctor and another consulting physician have concluded that it is medically improbable that I will recover, I hereby declare that no life-prolonging measures shall be taken or shall be stopped when it is clear such measures will only prolong the process of dying. I wish to die naturally, only taking those medications that will make me comfortable.

This declaration shall be honored by my family and my doctor, as it is the final expression of my legal rights to refuse treatment and to accept the consequences of that refusal.

If it has been determined that I am unable to express my wishes regarding the withdrawal of life-sustaining measures, I hereby designate ______________________________ as my surrogate to carry out my wishes, as stated in this declaration.

Print the name, address, and telephone number of your surrogate.

Name: ____

Address: ____

Zip Code: ____

Phone: ____

If my appointed surrogate does not wish or for some reason cannot act on my behalf, I hereby designate ______________________________ as my alternative surrogate, who will carry out the provisions of this declaration.

Print name, address, and telephone number of your alternative surrogate.

Name: ____

Address: ____

Zip Code:____

Phone: ____

Additional Instructions

____

____

____

____

____

____

____

____

____

I understand the contents and consequences of this declaration, and I am emotionally and mentally able to make this declaration.

Signed:__________________________________ Date: __________

Two witnesses must sign their names and print their addresses.

Witness #1

Signed:____

Address: ____

Witness #2

Signed: ____

Address:____

Designation of Health Care Surrogate

Name: ____
Last First M.I.

If it has been determined that I am unable to make informed decisions regarding my medical treatment and procedures, I hereby designate ______________________ as my surrogate for health care decisions.

Print the name, home address, and telephone number of your surrogate.

Name: ____

Address: ____

Zip Code: ____

Phone: ____

If for some reason my surrogate does not wish to or cannot act in my best interest, I hereby designate______________________________ as my alternative surrogate.

Print the name, address, and telephone number of your alternative surrogate.

Name: ____

Address: ____

Zip Code: ____

Phone: ____

I completely understand that this declaration allows my surrogate to make health care decisions for me, to search for public benefits to defray health care costs, and to approve my admission to or transfer from a health care facility.

Add any personal instructions here if you so wish.

____

____

____

Additional Instructions

I also confirm that this declaration is not being made as a condition of treatment or admission to a health care facility. I will inform and send a copy of this document to ____________________________________ so they are aware who my surrogate is.

Print the names and addresses of two people you want to keep copies of this document.

Name:____

Address: ____

Name: ____

Address:____

Sign and date the document.

Signed: ______________________________ Date: __________

(Two witnesses must sign their names and print their addresses)

Witness #1

Signed: ____

Address:____

Witness #2

Signed: ____

Address:____

Power of Attorney

This is a warning to the person executing this document:

This is an important legal document that is authorized by the laws of this state. The powers designated in this document are extensive and comprehensive. They are defined in ______________________ (*state laws*) of the ______________ (*your state*) laws.

Using this form is voluntary and ____________________ (*state laws*) allows the use of any other form of power of attorney if both parties involved agree.

I, ____________________________________ (*name and address*) hereby designate ____________________________ (*name and address*) my attorney-in-fact.

First

In my name, act in any way that I myself would if I were actually present, with regard to the following matters:

Here, strike out and initial any of the subdivisions that you do not want to give your attorney-in-fact authority for. If any of the subdivisions are eliminated, this automatically eliminates Subdivision J.

You must cross out the subdivision and initial it.

(A) Real Estate Transactions

(B) Chattel and Goods Transactions

(C) Bond, Share, and Commodity Transactions

(D) Banking Transactions

(E) Business Operating Transactions

(F) Insurance Transactions

(G) Claims and Litigations

(H) Benefits from Military Service

(I) Reports, Records, and Statements

(J) All Other Matters

You may include special directives here, but only if they conform to your state's power of attorney requirements.

Second

This power of attorney will:

(A) Be of indefinite duration

(B) End on ____________________ (*date*), unless otherwise ended

Third

This confirms all that the attorney-in-fact should do.

I hereby witness and sign my name on this ______________________ day of ____________________________________ 20 _____.

Name:____

Acknowledgment: Let it be known that this designation will not by affected by the ineptitude of the recipient.

I hereby witness and sign my name on this ______________________ day of ____________________________________ 20 _____.

Name:____

Acknowledgment: This document shall by recorded or filed by the two clerks or recorders of deeds.

Considerations in Planning Your Estate

Personal Information

Name:____

Social Security Number: __________________________________

Are You a U.S. Citizen: O Yes O No

Current Address: ______________________________________

Phone Number: _______________________________________

E-mail: ____

Marital Status

O Single, Never Married
O Married Once (Spouse still alive)
O Window/Widower
O Presently Married (Had prior marriage)
O Divorced

(If Married) Name of Spouse: ______________________________

Spouse's Social Security Number: __________________________

Is Spouse a U.S. Citizen: O Yes O No

Children

How many children do you have (including stepchildren and adopted children)? ________

If you have stepchildren or adopted children, do you wish to treat them the same as your biological children? O Yes O No

Is any child a minor? O Yes O No

Value of Estate

The value of your estate determines which is the appropriate will for you. Your estate value includes the value of all the property owned in your name and, if married, the value of property in your spouse's name. If any value has a debt, be sure to include that value. Also, list the value of any life insurance policies that you may have. *Please note that your life insurance usually does not pass according to your will, but it will be distributed to the beneficiaries whom you have listed on the policy.*

Approximate value of your estate (not including life insurance):

$ ______________________

Approximate value of your spouse's estate (not including life insurance):

$ ______________________

Value of life insurance (self and spouse):

$ ______________________

Total value of combined estates, including life insurance:

$ ______________________

Please note that if you think the value of your estate is more than $1 million, it may incur estate taxes. Also note that advanced planning can help you decrease your estate tax.

Family Farms & Family Businesses

Do you have a family farm? O Yes O No

Do you have a family business? O Yes O No

Real Estate

Usually, a husband and wife own real estate together and have right of survivorship. *Please note that if you and your spouse jointly own your real estate, then your will should not affect how your ownership passes when you die.*

Do you own real estate jointly with your spouse?

O Yes O No

Do you own real estate other than jointly with your spouse?

O Yes O No

If yes, how do you wish to allot your property?

O All to spouse

O To pass with the rest of estate

O My home to my spouse, and the rest of my real estate to pass with the rest of my estate

O My home to my spouse as long as my spouse lives; then, my home and the rest of my real estate to pass with the rest of my estate

O Different properties to different beneficiaries *(Please list below each property and to whom you are leaving it and what that person's relationship is to you)*

____

____

____

Personal Items & Tangible Property

How do you wish to give your personal items? *Please be sure to attach a detailed list of all personal items and note which item is to pass to various individuals if you wish to divide your estate as such.*

- O All to spouse
- O Specific items to specific individuals, with items not listed to go to my spouse
- O Specific items to go to specific individuals, with items not listed to pass with the rest of my estate
- O Everything to pass with rest of my estate
- O Other *(Explain below)*

____

____

____

Specific Bequests

Please note that while you may give specific gifts of cash, real estate, and/or personal property to individual people or charities in your will, these bequests will be allotted first, which may greatly deplete the value of your estate. If certain listed items cannot be found at your death, then probate of your estate may be complicated. Thus, you should only make bequests of property or cash that you will be sure that you will have when you die. If you choose not to make specific bequests, all of your estate property will pass to your indicated primary beneficiaries. Please note that many states require you to make a "personal memorandum" in which you can make individual bequests separate from your will. However, while these gifts are not always legally binding in most states, your executor will give as much credit to these gifts as your state law allows.

Do you wish to make any specific bequest(s) in your will?

O Yes O No

____

____

____

Residuary Estate

This includes whatever property is left over after paying for all your incurred debts, specific bequests, and the expense of administration. This is typically the property left to your beneficiaries, as many people do not make specific bequests.

To whom do you want to leave your residuary estate?

O All to my spouse if he/she survives me and, if not, then to my children

O A minimum bequest to my spouse, disinheriting him/her to the fullest extent of the law, with the remainder of my estate to be distributed to other person(s)

O All to one specific beneficiary other than my spouse

O To more than one beneficiary

If you have more than one beneficiary, are they:

O Specific people who are to share equally

O A group of people described as a class to share equally (e.g., my sisters)

O Some other unequal division between the beneficiaries (e.g.: 75% to one beneficiary and 25% to the other)

O Other *(Please explain below)*

____

____

____

If any of your beneficiaries is a minor, at what age would you like for them to receive their gift?

O 18

O 21

O Other Age: _______________

Please note that if you decide to select an age older than 21, the specific request will likely require a trust. A trust may cause your estate to have additional expenses for the future administration of the trust, which would lower the amount available for your beneficiaries.

Executor

Your executor, or personal representative, is appointed to ensure that your estate is settled when you die. This process will typically involve going through probate, which is a court-administered procedure designed to settle an estate as provided in your will or by the state law. The process of probate involves petitioning a court for letters of appointment, settling creditor claims, finding and distributing assets, and filing any necessary tax returns. While any adult may serve as your executor, some states would prefer you to have an executor who is a legal resident of the state where the probate will occur.

Whom do you wish to serve as your executor?

- O Spouse
- O My spouse and a co-executor
- O My spouse and a successor executor
- O One executor other than my spouse
- O Two co-executors, neither of whom are my spouse*
- O One executor and a successor executor, neither of whom are my spouse.**

**Usually, this option is not recommended because conflicts often arise between the executors, which will complicate the administration of your estate.*

***The successor will act only if your first choice cannot be the executor.*

If you wish for someone other than your spouse to be your executor, please list that person(s) below:

____

____

____

Guardian

If you have children who are minors when you die, and their other natural parent is not alive or cannot become their guardian, the court will typically appoint the person whom you name in your will to serve as your children's legal guardian until they reach the legal age of 18. If you are divorced, the court will typically grant custody of your children to the child's natural parent, even if you state otherwise in your will. However, be sure to name a guardian in the case that child's other natural parent dies before you.

Do you wish to appoint:

- O One guardian for my child
- O One guardian and a successor guardian
- O Two co-guardians
- O No guardian

Please list the name, relationship, and address of the person whom you wish to appoint guardianship.

1st Choice: ______________________________________

2nd Choice: ______________________________________

3rd Choice: ______________________________________

Trusts

You can set up a trust to skip giving your estate directly to your beneficiary. With a trust, you can give your estate to a trustee for the benefit of your beneficiary until he or she reaches the age of your designation, (such as 20, 25, 30, etc.). Under the directions that you outline in the trust, the trustee will manage your estate under court supervision. While the primary purpose of the trustee is to safeguard the inheritance, the inheritance can also be used for your beneficiary's health, education, or welfare at the trustee's discretion. You also have the option to create a trust to pool your estate, which means that your estate will remain in a single trust until all beneficiaries reach the age of your designation. Here, the trustee still has the ability to apply funds to each beneficiary as he or she has a need, which may lead to not all beneficiaries receiving the same amount of funds. This type of trust could be useful if you foresee some beneficiaries needing more financial assistance over a longer period of time. A trust will also protect your estate from third parties who may have a claim against one of your beneficiaries.

However, trusts are unnecessary because your gifts to beneficiaries under 18 (or, if you prefer, 21) will be controlled by your executor and then guardian after probate. This is possible because of the Uniform Gifts to Minors Act. While still allowing the guardian to use the funds in necessary situations, this act eliminates the need for a trust unless you perhaps have beneficiaries who are disabled, beneficiaries from a prior marriage, or if you have a large estate. Thus, a trust is worth the further complication if you wish for a guardian to spend more money on one child than another (e.g., a child with special needs).

Do you want a trust?

O Yes O No

If yes, would this be:

- O One trust for the benefit of all beneficiaries ("pooled" trust)
- O Individual trusts for each of the beneficiaries

At what age do you want your beneficiaries to be when the trust ends?

- O 18
- O 21
- O Other Age: ______________

Name of Trustee (*Please indicate below, along with his or her relationship to you)*

1st Choice: ____

2nd Choice: ____

3rd Choice: ____

Do you want the trustee to have the power to dissolve the trust if it becomes unfeasible to maintain?

- O Yes *(Note: The inherited property will remain under the guardian's control if the child is a minor at the time of the trust's termination)*
- O No

Do you want the trustee to exercise the power to terminate the trust if it falls below a specific amount?

O Yes O No

If yes, then what amount? $ ______________

Disinheriting Someone

Do you wish to disinherit someone other than your spouse?

O Yes O No

If so, please indicate who as well as his or her relationship to you:

____

Do you wish to disinherit anyone who contests your will?

O Yes O No

Do you wish to have your executor distribute your estate, either outright or in trust, if you chose to disinherit your spouse? This may minimize any "right of election" that your spouse may have under the laws of jurisdiction.

O Yes O No

Please note that some states provide a spouse a "right of election," which would grant him or her the ability to apply the state law instead of what you wish in your will.

Distribution of Estate to Children

Do you wish for a minor's gifts to be:

- O Paid at the election of the executor
- O Held in trust until the child reaches legal age

If you have adopted or stepchildren, do you:

- O Include them in your will the same as your natural children
- O Exclude them from your will
- O Have the will remain silent in regard to adopted and stepchildren

Do you have a child who is adopted or a stepchild?

O Yes O No

Name: ____

How do you wish for him or her to be treated in your will?

____

____

List all the names of your children:

____

____

Primary Beneficiaries

Whom do you wish to receive all or the majority of your estate?

- O My spouse, if he or she survives me, and if not, then my children
- O Disinherit spouse (to the fullest extent of the law)
- O My children
- O My parents in equal shares, or if not, then my siblings in equal shares

  List names and relationships

  ____

  ____

- O To these beneficiaries *(List name, relationship, and estate percentage)*

  ____

  ____

If, for some reason, any of the before-mentioned beneficiaries die before you and leave descendents, do you want the share of the deceased beneficiary to pass to their children, or would you like your estate to pass only to the beneficiaries named above?

- O Allow estate to pass to the children of any deceased beneficiary
- O Allow estate to only pass to the named beneficiaries listed

If, for some reason, all your named beneficiaries either die before you or die within 30 days after you, please list those to whom you wish to leave your estate. Remember to provide his or her name, relationship, and percentage of your estate that you wish to leave them.

___

___

___

Living Will and Health Care

Though a living will is a separate document from your will, it may be an important part of your estate plan. The living will provides instructions for your family and executor on what to do if you suffer an incurable medical condition or if you become incapacitated. This document directs doctors on how to care for you. You can provide specific details in your will to indicate the specific conditions that need to occur to activate it. Remember, once you activate it, it is in effect until you revoke it, which you can do at any time by either telling someone who can testify that you wanted to revoke it or by physically destroying it. However, this document only addresses continued life support if you have a terminable condition. For other situations, you will need a power of attorney for health care.

Do you want a living will?

O Yes O No

Another separate document, though equally important, is a special power of attorney who you grant for health care. You may execute this power of attorney in addition to or in lieu of your living will. It will appoint someone that you designate to make any medical care decisions for you if you are incapable of making your own decisions. This document provides for more situations than a living will. This will grant your power of attorney to make medical decisions on your behalf and also will allow him or her access to your medical records in order to make those decisions.

Do you want a health care power of attorney?

O Yes O No

Do you want your spouse to act as your agent if he or she is alive?

O Yes O No

If you do not wish for your spouse to act as your agent, please provide the name and address of the person whom you wish to grant medical power of attorney to:

____

Do you wish to donate your organs for transplant once you die? *(Please note that this information can often be found on your driver's license, as well)*

O Yes O No

If you answered yes, are you also willing to donate your organs for medical, educational, or scientific purposes?

O Yes O No

Would you prefer to die at home rather than in the hospital, assuming that this does not place a burden upon your family?

O Yes O No

Springing Durable General Power of Attorney

While your will allows you control of the distribution of your property after you die, you are in control of your property while you are alive, as long as you are of sound mind. However, if for some reason you become incapacitated, a court may revoke your right to manage your own affairs and grant the right to a guardian that the court appoints. You can appoint your own agent instead of the court's by granting someone you trust power of attorney.

A power of attorney authorizes another person to make decisions and act on your behalf. While a normal power of attorney becomes null and void when you are deemed mentally disabled, a springing durable power of attorney would actually take effect at this time. This power of attorney would last as long as you are alive, or until you chose to revoke it. However, remember to name someone as your attorney in fact because your power of attorney will have a strong authority over your affairs, and while he or she may use it effectively, this power is also easily abused.

Would you like to have a springing durable power of attorney?

O Yes O No

Would you like your spouse to act as your agent?

O Yes O No

If you elect someone other than your spouse to act on your behalf, please list his or her name and his or her relationship to you below:

____

Funeral Arrangements

Perhaps you have an idea of how you wish your funeral to be performed. It is essential to communicate your wishes with your family and friends prior to your death because if you keep your wishes detailed in a letter of instruction that accompanies your will, these instructions may not be read until after your burial.

At my death, I would like:

- O To be cremated
- O To have my body donated for scientific or medical purposes
- O To be buried at a specific grave site or location *(Please list below)*

  ____

- O To be buried at sea
- O To be buried with full military honors *(Please also select another option in addition to this one)*
- O Other: ______________________________________
- O I would prefer this decision to be made by those who survive me

Your Financial Data

Please keep in mind that if your estate exceeds $1 million total, then you may be subject to estate taxes and should consult your attorney.

1) Determining the Value of Your Assets

Please provide the numerical values in the chart. You only need to provide approximate figures if you do not know the actual value of your assets. Make sure that you have proof of ownership for any property requiring such.

	Joint	You	Spouse	Total
Checking Accounts				
Savings Accounts				
Money Market Accounts				
Stocks				
Bonds				
Mutual Funds				
Residence Equity				
Other Real Estate Equity				
Investments (Including Retirement)				
Closely Held Businesses				
Life Insurance				
Vehicles				
Furniture				
Jewelry				
Artwork & Antiques				
Electronics				
Other Personal Property				

	Joint	You	Spouse	Total
Other Assets				
Other Assets				
Other Assets				
Other Assets				
Total				

In the past, have you ever filed an IRS Form 709 "A U.S. Gift Tax Return"?

O Yes *(Please provide copy)* O No

2) Residence Information

A) Primary Residence (*Please list your address below):*

____

____

Estimated Value	Amount of Mortgages	Equity	Monthly Mortgage Payment	Owned By

Please provide a copy of the deed and mortgages to allow for an expedited disbursement.

Original Purchase Price: $ ________________

Cost of Additional Improvements: $ ________________

How long do you plan on remaining at this residence? ________________

What do you plan on doing with the property? ____________________

B) Secondary Residence (*Please list your address below):*

____

____

Estimated Value	Amount of Mortgages	Equity	Monthly Mortgage Payment	Owned By

Please provide a copy of the deed and mortgages to allow for an expedited disbursement.

Original Purchase Price: $ ______________

Cost of Additional Improvements: $ ______________

How long do you plan on keeping this residence? ______________

What do you plan on doing with the property? ____________________

Do you rent this residence?

O Yes O No

3) Investment Account Information (Not including retirement accounts)

A) Jointly owned investment accounts in your and your spouse's name:

Location	Estimated Value	Amount of Margin Loans	Net Value	Other Co-Owners
Total				

B) Investment accounts that you alone own:

Location	Estimated Value	Amount of Margin Loans	Net Value	Other Co-Owners
Total				

C) Investment accounts that only your spouse owns:

Location	Estimated Value	Amount of Margin Loans	Net Value	Other Co-Owners
Total				

4) Retirement Benefits

A) List your retirement benefits:

Description	Current Value	Beneficiary
Total		

B) List your spouse's retirement benefits:

Description	Current Value	Beneficiary
Total		

C) Provide any other pertinent retirement account information:

____

____

5) Liability Information

A) Joint liabilities:

Creditor	Liability Amount	Payment Amount	Payment Frequency	Secured
Total				

B) Your sole liabilities, other than previously listed:

Creditor	Liability Amount	Payment Amount	Payment Frequency	Secured
Total				

C) Your spouse's liabilities, other than those previously listed:

Creditor	Liability Amount	Payment Amount	Payment Frequency	Secured
Total				

6) Life Insurance Information

A) Life insurance policies (*Please list both yours and your spouse's*):

Company	Type	Face Amount (Death Benefit)	Cash Surrender Value	Beneficiary
Total				

B) List only your life insurance policies:

Company	Type	Face Amount (Death Benefit)	Cash Surrender Value	Beneficiary
Total				

C) List only your spouse's life insurance policies:

Company	Type	Face Amount (Death Benefit)	Cash Surrender Value	Beneficiary
Total				

D) Please list any other vital information concerning you or your spouse's life insurance policies that may be helpful to your executor:

Tentative Tax

The tax base is the sum of the taxable estate and the adjusted taxable gifts, which are taxable gifts made after 1976. The tentative tax is then calculated by applying the following tax rates:

Amount	Tax
<$10,000	18%
$10,000 - $20,000	$1,800 + 20% of excess over $10,000
$20,001 - $40,000	$3,800 + 22% of excess over $20,000
$40,001 - $60,000	$8,200 + 24% of excess over $40,000
$60,001 - $80,000	$13,000 + 26% of excess over $60,000
$80,001 - $100,000	$18,200 + 28% of excess over $80,000
$100,001 - $150,000	$23,800 + 30% of excess over $100,000
$150,001 - $250,000	$38,800 + 32% of excess over $150,000
$250,001 - $500,000	$70,800 + 34% of excess over $250,000
$500,001 - $750,000	$155,800 + 27% of excess over $500,000
$750,001 - $1,000,000	$248,300 + 39% of excess over $750,000

The Complete Guide to Organizing Your Records for Estate Planning

Step-by-Step Instructions With Companion CD-ROM

The Complete Guide to Organizing Your Records for Estate Planning is your comprehensive toolkit for gathering all your estate planning documents and records — before you visit an attorney. Planning your estate is a long, complicated process that requires much time and effort. The process of organizing your records for estate planning is equally time consuming and complex. With the help of this book, you can take on the first estate planning steps yourself, saving time and avoiding costly attorney fees.

ISBN 9781601382351

If you found *The Complete Guide to Planning Your Estate in Virginia* helpful, check out Atlantic Publishing Group, Inc.'s other title *The Complete Guide to Organizing Your Records for Estate Planning*. This new book is packed full of charts and worksheets to help you organize all your personal documents, records, and essential information. Use this book to create your estate planning portfolio before visiting an estate planning attorney to save time, thus saving money on costly attorney fees.

The following appendix provides a sneak peek at this new book, providing you with additional checklists, sample templates, and worksheets to help you plan your estate portfolio. When you purchase the hard copy of the book, you will receive a CD-ROM filled with all of the worksheets you see here and many more. The CD-ROM makes it easy to organize your information and print the worksheets from your home computer. Order *The Complete Guide to Organizing Your Records for Estate Planning* today!

To order visit:
www.atlantic-pub.com
***Or order toll-free:* 800-814-1132**

Appendix C

How Much Do You Know About Estate Planning?

If you think you know everything about estate planning, then I invite you to take the quiz below. If you are like most people, you may not know as much as you think, and what you do not know can cost you and your family thousands of dollars. Worse than that, it can add to your family's stress during a time when they may be emotionally overwrought.

Estate Planning Quiz

You will have a number of True/False (T/F) questions, multiple-choice questions, and fill-in-the-blank questions.

1. Estate planning requires an attorney.
   ❑ *True* ❑ *False*

2. You are required to be embalmed when you are being buried.
   ❑ *True* ❑ *False*

3. You are required to buy a casket at the funeral home you have chosen to use.

   ❑ *True* ❑ *False*

4. If you are cremated, you are not allowed to have your ashes scattered in a public place.

   ❑ *True* ❑ *False*

5. If you have property transferred to a trust, it must still go through probate.

   ❑ *True* ❑ *False*

6. There is no such thing as an oral will.

   ❑ *True* ❑ *False*

7. You have to pay taxes on any monetary gifts you give, no matter the amount.

   ❑ *True* ❑ *False*

8. A doctor has to follow your medical directives.

   ❑ *True* ❑ *False*

9. A will must be typed and signed in order to be valid.

   ❑ *True* ❑ *False*

10. You must state whom you want as a guardian in your will.

    ❑ *True* ❑ *False*

11. Once you have your will and durable power of attorney done, regardless of where you may move, it is valid in all 50 states and the District of Columbia.

    ❑ *True* ❑ *False*

12. A _______ proceeding is required with a will.
    A. trust
    B. will
    C. probate
    D. none of the above

13. A(n) ______ is a trust that allows you to bypass probate hearings concerning a particular property.
    A. Irrevocable Land Trust
    B. Revocable Living Trust
    C. Time Stamped Trust
    D. none of the above

14. The creation of a _______ is possible with the carbon from cremation ashes.
    A. model
    B. diamond
    C. clone
    D. none of the above

15. You can ____ a casket for a viewing.
    A. steal
    B. hang
    C. rent
    D. none of the above

16. You can lose around _____ percent of your property in probate hearings.
    A. 20
    B. 50
    C. 75
    D. none of the above

17. A _____ is a type of fraternal membership.
    A. Water Buffalo Order
    B. Jaycee
    C. Freemason
    D. none of the above

18. A(n) ________ is another name for a handwritten will.
    A. laser
    B. holographic
    C. ethical
    D. none of the above

19. You can put a body ______ instead of embalming.
    A. on ice
    B. in a special chemical soup
    C. there is no substitute
    D. none of the above

20. A _____ is a large party to celebrate a person's life.
    A. wake
    B. visitation
    C. viewing
    D. none of the above

21. A ______ allows you to name someone while you are alive to take care of your financial matters, should you become incapacitated.
    A. medical power of attorney
    B. durable power of attorney for finances
    C. revocable living trust
    D. none of the above

22. A(n) __________ is a set of instructions of what to do if you should become incapacitated and unable to make medical decisions.

23. A(n) ________ is in charge of handling your affairs after you die.

24. A(n) ______ agreement occurs before a couple is married and can impact a person's estate.

25. A(n) _______ trust allows a couple to pass on their estate only after both spouses have died. It is a trust that helps prevent federal estate taxes from being levied.

26. It is a good idea to assign someone to care for your pet. There are some _________ schools that will take them in and take care of them.

27. What assets escape probate without any real action on your part? ____

28. _________ donation can be done for medical research at a university.

29. A(n) ________ is a place where urns can be stored.

30. A(n)________ account is a bank account that can allow funds to be released upon your death.

31. A(n)________ is someone who is chosen to carry a casket.

32. Being ________ is a state in which you cannot make decisions for yourself.

33. Does everyone pay estate taxes?

34. Can I simply gift away all my possessions before I die?

35. Is it possible to make a change to an Irrevocable Trust that has already been established?

36. Can a parent sign legal documents, handle business affairs, or make medical decisions for their adult children?

37. For Medicaid purposes, is a transfer of not more than $12,000 annually allowed?

38. Does a will completely avoid probate?

39. If both parents die, and there are minor children, who has priority for the judge to pick as guardian?

A Letter to Those You Love

The letter you write in this section should be the first thing your loved ones read, should you become incapacitated in some way or die. Though it is the first thing in the portfolio, it will actually be the last thing you do while preparing your estate portfolio. It is one of the most important items, so take your time creating your letter.

Your letter will serve a few different purposes. One purpose is that it is the instruction manual for using your portfolio. It will also contain special messages to your loved ones and words of comfort. It may contain your thoughts on death and dying, and your last thoughts and words for the world to hear.

To help you create your own letter, below you will find a simple template of the sections of your letter. This can be a difficult and emotional task for some people. Have the thoughts you want to be included, and you can direct these words to one person, or a select group of people. It can be as simple or elaborate as you choose. Just make sure it is purposeful and meaningful, and expresses the things you want to say to your loved ones at the time when they need to hear your words the most.

Dear ________________ ,

Why: This is an explanation of why they are reading this letter, such as, you have died or have become incapacitated.

My Instructions: In this section, you will describe how to use the portfolio and what its purpose is. The section should contain step-by-step instructions that are easy to read, understand, and execute. Be detailed and structured in your instructions.

Death: In this section, you will describe your feelings and ideas about life, death, and the afterlife. You should talk about your hopes and fears concerning these subjects. Allow those who read this to find comfort that you will be all right and in a better state. You can talk about looking forward to meeting loved ones who have passed before you or about your religious visions of the afterlife.

Messages: In this section, you will write to specific people who are important to you. These are messages and words of love and comfort that you are leaving behind. Make sure they are personal and from your heart.

Last Thoughts: In this section, you will have some last words and thoughts as you pass from this world. You can use a quote or create words of your own. These are your final thoughts for the world to hear.

____

Signature

If you do not feel comfortable writing a letter, you can create an audio or visual letter to your loved ones. There are books at your local library or bookstore that talk about creating last letters and love letters to your family and friends.

Biography

In the biography section of your portfolio, you will include all the important information about your life. It will have a fact sheet that contains all your vital information. This sheet will be used considerably by your loved ones, so make sure it is always accurate and up-to-date.

My Fact Sheet

Name	Address	Years at this Address
Date of Birth	Telephone Number	Social Security Number
Mother's Maiden Name		Driver's License Number
Employer	Employer Address	Employer Phone Number

My Children

Name		
Address		
Phone Number		

My Spouse

Name	Address	Phone Number
Date of Birth	Date of Marriage	Date of Death

My Physician

Type of Doctor			
Name			
Phone Number			
Prescribed Medications			

My Biographical Information

Full Name (including middle and maiden names)
Date of Birth

Place of Birth
Social Security Number
Driver's License Number
Other Names Known By

My Military Record

Military Service (branch, location, and rank)	Military Service (branch, location, and rank)	Military Service (branch, location, and rank)	Military Service (branch, location, and rank)
Dates Served	Dates Served	Dates Served	Dates Served
Military Honors	Military Honors	Military Honors	Military Honors

My Biological Parents

My Biological Mother

Name (including maiden name)	Address
Birth Date	Phone Number
Place of Birth	Date of Death
Military Service (branch, location, and rank)	Military Honors

My Biological Father

Name	Address
Birth Date	Phone Number
Place of Birth	Date of Death
Military Service (branch, location, and rank)	Military Honors

My Stepparents (If Applicable)

My Stepmother

Name (including maiden name)	Address
Birth Date	Phone Number
Place of Birth	Date of Death
Military Service (branch, location, and rank)	Military Honors

My Stepfather

Name	Address
Birth Date	Phone Number
Place of Birth	Date of Death
Military Service (branch, location, and rank)	Military Honors

My Prior Marriages (If Applicable)

1st Marriage

Name (including maiden name)	Address
Birth Date	Phone Number
Place of Birth	Date of Death
Date of Marriage	Date of Divorce or Separation

2nd Marriage

Name (including maiden name)	Address
Birth Date	Phone Number
Place of Birth	Date of Death
Date of Marriage	Date of Divorce or Separation

3rd Marriage

Name (including maiden name)	Address
Birth Date	Phone Number
Place of Birth	Date of Death
Date of Marriage	Date of Divorce or Separation

My Current Spouse or Long-Term Partner

Name (including maiden name)	Address
Birth Date	Phone Number
Place of Birth	Date of Death
Date of Marriage	Date of Divorce or Separation

My Employment

Name of Employer	Address	Phone Number
Date Employed	Date Retired	Contact Person
If two employers, complete form below:		
Name of Employer	Address	Phone Number
Date Employed	Date Retired	Contact Person

My Children

Child 1

Name	Address
Birth Date	Phone Number
Place of Birth	Date of Death
Military Service (branch, location, and rank)	Military Honors

Child 2

Name	Address
Birth Date	Phone Number
Place of Birth	Date of Death
Military Service (branch, location, and rank)	Military Honors

Child 3

Name	Address
Birth Date	Phone Number
Place of Birth	Date of Death
Military Service (branch, location, and rank)	Military Honors

My Grandchildren

Name	Address
Birth Date	Phone Number
Place of Birth	Date of Death
Military Service (branch, location, and rank)	Military Honors

My Siblings

Name	Address
Birth Date	Phone Number
Place of Birth	Date of Death
Military Service (branch, location, and rank)	Military Honors

My Nieces or Nephews

Name	Address
Birth Date	Phone Number
Place of Birth	Date of Death
Military Service (branch, location, and rank)	Military Honors

Name	Address
Birth Date	Phone Number
Place of Birth	Date of Death
Military Service (branch, location, and rank)	Military Honors

Other Important People to Notify

Name	Address
Relation	Phone Number
Name	Address
Relation	Phone Number
Name	Address
Relation	Phone Number

People Who Should Not Be Contacted

Name	Reason Not to Notify
Name	Reason Not to Notify

Care of Others

Information about Adults Who Rely on Me

This is a list of people I care for in various functions. Please help make sure they are cared for, and contact the person I have named as a caregiver.

Name Phone Number		Address
DOB	My Relationship to the Person	

Type of Care I Provide
Contact Information of Appointed Caregiver

Name Phone Number		Address
DOB	My Relationship to the Person	
Type of Care I Provide		
Contact Information of Appointed Caregiver		

Name Phone Number		Address
DOB	My Relationship to the Person	
Type of Care I Provide		
Contact Information of Appointed Caregiver		

Additional Caregivers

The following is a list of people who also provide care for the individuals listed above.

Person's Name	Caregiver's Contact Information	Relationship to Person	Type of Care They Provide

My Pets

Pet Care Instructions

Pet's Name, Species, and Identifying Marks	Location of Animal	Food and Water Regimen
Health and Other Care Instructions	**Person I Name to Care for My Pet and their Contact Information**	**Veterinarian's Name and Number**

My Employment

My Employment Information

Upon my incapacitation or death, please contact my current employers, below. You should ask about any benefits, pensions, or insurance that I may have, but may have failed to record here. Please determine whether there are any unpaid wages or commissions, expense reimbursements, or bonuses that may be due to my estate.

Employer's Contact Information	Current Benefits	
	My Position	
	Start Date	
	Ownership Interest	❑ Yes (%) ❑ No
Employer's Contact Information	Current Benefits	

	My Position	
	Start Date	
	Ownership Interest	❑ Yes (%) ❑ No

My Previous Jobs

(This section needs only to be filled out if you receive benefits from that company.)

Employer's Contact Information	Current Benefits	
	My Position	
	Start Date	End Employment Date
	Ownership Interest	❑ Yes (%) ❑ No

Employer's Contact Information	Current Benefits	
	My Position	
	Start Date	End Employment Date
	Ownership Interest	❑ Yes (%) ❑ No

Employer's Contact Information	Current Benefits

	My Position	
	Start Date	End Employment Date
	Ownership Interest	❑ Yes (%) ❑ No

My Business Ownership

The information contained in this section relates to my business interests. Specifically, it deals with information about whom to contact in the event of my death or if I should become incapacitated. This information can also be used to help you manage or sell my business interests.

Current Business Interests

These are businesses I currently own or have interest in.

Name and Location

Name of Business	Location and Telephone of Business	Where to Find Documents Related to Business

Ownership

Who Owns the Business	Address and Phone Number of Owner	Owner's Job Title or Position	What Percentage They Own

These are businesses I currently own or have interest in.

Name and Location

Directions Concerning Disposition of Entire Business			
Directions Concerning My Interest			
Contact Information for Key Individuals			
Name	Position	Contact Information	Their Role in Business
Disposition Documents			
Tax ID Number			
State ID Number			

Employees

This section deals with the people who are key in keeping my business running.

Employee Name	Type of Agreement They Have with Company	Benefits	Contact Information

Business Taxes

Tax Record Information

Current-Year Records	Location of Documents
	Who is Responsible for Documents
Prior-Year Records	Location of Documents
	Who is Responsible for Documents

Assets and Liabilities

This section lists assets and liabilities. This information is intended to help manage, transfer, or sell the business.

Assets

Description of Particular Asset	Current Location of Asset	Value of Asset	Contact Name and Information	Location of Asset Documents

Liabilities

Description of Particular Asset	Current Location of Asset	Value of Asset	Contact Name and Information	Location of Asset Documents

Answers to the Estate Planning Quiz

Here you will find the answers to the questions in the beginning of this Appendix.

1. **F** While it does not require one, there are some aspects in which an attorney is recommended.

2. **F** There is no federal law that requires that a body be embalmed. Putting a body in a freezer will preserve it for a few days until a funeral.

3. **F** There is no law requiring you to buy anything from a funeral home. While they offer such items as caskets, you are not required to buy them.

4. **F** You may want to check with local laws, but you are allowed to scatter them in most public places.

5. **F** This allows you to bypass probate.

6. **F** There is an oral will, but it is not as binding as a signed one and can lead to problems in some areas and states.

7. **F** It must be over a certain amount before you pay taxes on the money.

8. **F** They may refuse to follow the directives, but you would then get a new doctor.

9. **F** It can be oral, but it is not recommended.

10. **F** If you do not, the court system will choose one for your children.

11. **F** Every state has specific rules. A will or a durable power of attorney that is valid in one state could be void in another. Check with an attorney in your new state.

12. C

13. B

14. B

15. C

16. D

17. C

18. B

19. A

20. A

21. B

22. Medical Directive

23. Executor

24. Marital or Prenuptial

25. AB

26. Veterinary

27. Real Estate, IRAs, and 401(k) plans, which pass by beneficiary designation under the plan itself; life insurance, which again passes by beneficiary designation together with any payable on death accounts, which would pass directly to whoever is designated as a beneficiary; as well as joint accounts, which would pass by right of survivorship to the designated survivor.

28. Whole Body

29. Columbarium

30. TOD or Transfer on Death

31. Pallbearer

32. Incapacitated

33. No. Estate taxes are only imposed on individuals who have estates sufficiently large to trigger the tax.

34. No. The estate tax is tied up with the gift tax so that if you gift all your belongings before death, you might end up paying the same in the gift tax as you would simply leaving your property alone.

35. Yes, there are various ways, including:

    - Petitioning the court to make the desired change.

    - Forming a new irrevocable trust with the desired change and having it purchase the assets from the existing irrevocable trust using an IOU that would be paid off at death, possibly from life insurance proceeds.

- When setting up an irrevocable trust, provide for a "protector" to be able to make a change. The protector cannot be the grantor, trustee, or beneficiary of the trust. It is someone who is named when the trust is formed and given the powers to make certain changes. Typically, you would name someone you trust, such as a family member (i.e., sister or brother) or a professional, such as your attorney or CPA. The protector cannot benefit themselves, but can only make changes as authorized by you, as grantor, when the trust is first established.

36. No. Once an individual reaches the age of majority (typically 18), the adult child should execute powers of attorney for financial and business affairs as well as their advanced legal directives. For example, an adult child heading off to college may want to execute the health care and financial documents so that if something happened to the child while at college, the parent would have the legal power to assist and make decisions.

37. No. The $12,000 annual gift tax exclusion is strictly a gift tax provision. Medicaid penalizes gifts of any size.

38. No. Not without a power of attorney, conservatorship, or letters testamentary.

39. Generally a grandparent. That knowledge alone could scare some people into getting their documents done.

Glossary of Terms

The many different terms used in estate planning are often confusing. Here are some that you need to take note of. These are simple, brief definitions of some terms you will find in this book. Make sure you consider that there might be differences in how they are used.

AB Trust. An AB trust is one that establishes two trusts, one for each spouse. The surviving spouse can then use the property in the other's trust, but avoids double taxation on the property from when one spouse dies to when the second spouse dies.

Abatement. This is the process of pulling back specific gifts under a will when it becomes necessary to create a fund to meet expenses or to pay taxes, or in other specific situations.

Abstract of Trust. This tool allows you to say that your trust exists and that it will be used. It is a "short list" of what is included in that trust, rather than spelling it all out.

Ademption. In ademption statues, laws are in place that protect heirs who do not or cannot receive what you leave to them in your will. If you leave property in your will and estate to someone, and that property is no longer part of your estate, this statute defines what should happen.

Basis. The tax basis is the value that is assigned to the property from which taxable gain or loss on a sale is determined. This means that when property is purchased, its basis tends to be the cost.

Beneficiary. A beneficiary is someone or a group who benefits from the gifts made under a legal document, which can include wills, trusts, pay-on-death accounts, retirement plans, and insurance products. This is the person who gets something from these documents.

Child's Trust. A trust that is created solely for the use of one child who is a minor.

Community Property. Property that is shared between you and your spouse, in a community living state. This property belongs equally to both parties, as it was obtained during the marriage.

Creditor. A company or an organization that is owed money; this is the company that lent you money that you need to repay.

Custodian. Under the Uniform Transfers to Minor Act, this is the person named by you to care for the property that is left to a minor child.

Death Taxes. Death taxes, probate taxes, or estate taxes are taxes that are assessed on the property of a person who has died.

Durable Power of Attorney. The power of attorney that remains effective even when the principal (person who created it) becomes incapacitated. This person is authorized to act in the other's place and is called an attorney in fact.

Estate. All the property that you own when you die is your estate. There are various ways of determining the value of your estate, as defined in this book, including your probate estate and your taxable estate.

Estate Planning. Planning for what will happen to your estate when you die while you are still alive. It helps you move your estate from your property to that of your heirs in the best manner possible.

Estate Taxes. These are taxes that are applied to your property when you die. There are various tax situations that you could be in; for example, the federal estate tax is levied when a person reaches the estate tax threshold for the year that they die.

Estate Tax Threshold. The dollar amount, as defined by the federal government, for the year that you die, at which point taxes are levied on your estate.

Executor. The individual who will manage your estate, move through probate, and collect all your assets. He or she will distribute them to your heirs as you define in your will.

Final Beneficiaries. Those people who will receive property from your estate.

Generation Skipping Trust. This is a trust that is set up to avoid double taxation. The principal leaves the trust for the grandchild, rather than for their children. This helps to avoid taxation from the principal to the child, and then again from the taxation when the child passes it to the grandchild.

Gifts. Property that is given to another person or organization. This can be done throughout life or through trusts, wills, and a living trust after death.

Gift Taxes. Taxes that are levied on any gifts when the gifts are given (usually before death).

Grantor. A grantor is a person who establishes a trust.

Health Care Directive. This document will define the wishes of the document writer in regard to health care when he or she cannot communicate those wishes themselves. It names a person who will make decisions for them at this time.

Heirs. Those who will inherit property, by law, at the time of death of those they are related to. Heirs will receive property that is not left specifically through a will or trust to someone else.

Holographic Will. Last will and testament completely written in the decedent's own handwriting, signed and dated but not required to be witnessed, legal only in those states that recognize such a will form.

Inheritance Taxes. Taxes that are imposed on property that is received by heirs at the time of death.

Insurance. A product that is purchased that provides protection from a variety of situations in the event that they happen. Life insurance, for example, provides coverage in a monetary benefit if the insured person dies while the policy is in effect.

International Will. Form of a will executed outside the United States and offered for probate in those states that recognize it.

Irrevocable Trust. A trust that can no longer be changed.

Joint Tenancy. When two or more people own property, the other will become the owner of the entire property when one dies.

Life Beneficiary. This inclusion in an AB trust allows for the other spouse to take use of the property in Trust A for his or her own needs, when one spouse dies. It does not provide ownership of this property to the spouse, though, which is the key factor in avoiding estate taxes.

Life Insurance Trust. This trust is one that owns a life insurance policy. It helps to reduce the size of the original owner's taxable estate.

Living Trust. A living trust is set up while the person is still alive, which still allows them to control what is in the trust until they die. It helps to minimize the value of property that ends up going through probate. Grantors are able to specify that the property in the trust will pass right to the beneficiaries at the time of death, avoiding probate.

Marital Deduction. In accordance with tax law, a marital deduction allows all property that is passed from one spouse to the other spouse at the time of death to be free from taxes.

Pay on Death. Variety of methods that are used for the payment of funds at the time of death. It defines who will acquire what remains in the account when the holder of the account dies.

Power of Attorney. The power of attorney provides legal documentation that the individual is giving authorization for someone other than themselves to act for them.

Probate. Probate is a process that includes several steps. Probate authenticates the will of the deceased, appoints the executor or administrator of your will, pays debts and taxes that are due on the estate, identifies who the heirs of the estate are, and distributes the property in the will to those who are designated in the will.

QTIP Trust. A Qualified Terminable Interest Property trust does not reduce or stop estate taxes, but it does postpone them. It can be used when an individual estate exceeds the estate tax threshold to postpone the payment of taxes on the estate.

Real Property. Real property is all land and all buildings attached to it, as well as all improvements made to it. It is real estate. Anything that is not real property is considered to be personal property.

Residual Beneficiary. A person who will receive property that is left in a will or trust that is not given to others in that document. It can also mean a person who receives property from a trust when the life beneficiary dies.

Right of Survivorship. When two people own property, this is the right that the joint tenant has in claiming the other's share of the property at the time of death.

Spoliated. Refers to a will that has been ruined in some way that makes it impossible to read, validate, or determine the wishes of the testator.

Successor Trustee. A successor trustee is a person whom the creator of the trust places in charge when he or she dies, if he or she is the trustee of the living trust.

Taxable Estate. This is the value of the estate that is able to be taxed, as it goes over the estate tax threshold or the allowable amount of no taxing.

Tenancy by the Entirety. This form of tenancy is one that is a form of marital property ownership. It provides joint ownership of property to both spouses.

Trust. A legal document and situation in which property is held for the benefit of others. The grantor or trustor places property into the trust that is managed by the trustee until it passes to the beneficiary.

Trustee. The trustee of a trust is the person who will manage the trust for the beneficiary until he or she can take claim to the property in it.

Trustor. The creator of a trust.

Uniform Transfers to Minors Act. This law provides for the method that property is transferred to minors in the event of a death.

Will. A will is a legal document that defines what the deceased person's wishes are in regard to his or her property. It provides for what their intentions are for where property should go after they die.

Bibliography

Campbell, Brett. Guide to Wills and Estates. 2nd ed. New York, NY: Random House, 2004.

Caverly, Brian N. and Jordan S. Simon. Estate Planning for Dummies. 1st ed. Indianapolis, IN: Wiley Publishing, 2003.

Clifford, Denis. Estate Planning Basics. 3rd ed. Berkeley, CA: Nolo, 2005.

Clifford, Denis and Cora Jordan. Plan Your Estate. 8th ed. Berkeley, CA: Nolo, 2006.

Esperti, Robert A. and Renno L. Peterson. Protect Your Estate. 2nd ed. New York, NY: McGraw-Hill, 2000.

"General Estate Planning." Wealthmangement.net. 18, Jan. 2007 **http://palmetto.forest.net/estateplan/customlc/look9/FMPro?-db=ads.fp5&-lay=Detail&-format=articlesdetail.htm&serial=1953&-token=5900&-find**.

Greenburg, Bernard H. "Estate Planning Practice in The Internet Age." LawGuru.com. June 2004. 20, Jan. 2007 **http://www.lawguru.com/articles/showarticle.php?id=38**.

Spencer, Patti S. Esq. Your Estate Matters. 1st ed. Bloomington, IN: Authorhouse, 2005.

Virginia Estate Planning Commission, **http://virginiaassetprotection.com/main_faqs.html#20**.

Virginia Probate Code, **http://law.justia.com/virginia/codes/toc6401000/toc6401000.html**.

Author Biographies

Sandy Baker

Sandy Baker is the mother of three and the wife of an amazing man. Together, they provide a range of helpful tools to help others to make their dreams and wishes come true. Estate planning is part of the tools that Sandy helps to present to others as a method of enriching their lives through leaving their legacy. With many years of professional writing experience, namely as a ghostwriter, she has written and researched the topic for many years, enhancing her ability to provide a thorough book for readers.

Linda C. Ashar, J.D.

Linda C. Ashar, J.D., is a lawyer, educator, horse breeder, freelance writer, and artist. Her law practice encompasses of more than 29 years before the Ohio and Federal Bars. She is a senior shareholder in the firm of Wickens, Herzer, Panza, Cook & Batista Co. in Avon, Ohio. In addition to her juris doctor in law, she has a Master of Arts in special education and Bachelor of Arts in English.

She is professional writer and has authored *101 Ways to Score Higher on Your LSAT: What You Need to Know About the Law School Admission Test Explained Simply* (Atlantic Publishing Group, Inc. 2008), poetry, and several magazine and journal articles.

She is an Adjunct Professor at DeVry University and a frequent speaker at law seminars.

She and her lawyer-husband, Mike, operate Thornapple Farms in Vermilion, Ohio, where they breed Morgan Horses, including rare Lippitt Morgan bloodstock, Connemara Ponies, and Irish Kerry Bog Ponies, a critically endangered breed. Ashar serves on several nonprofit boards and is co-founder of Elysian Fields: The Justin Morgan Association for Retired Equines and the American Kerry Bog Pony Society.

Her interpretive art has been showcased by Mac Worthington Gallery in Columbus, Ohio; she paints by private commission, subjects including equines, portraits, and landscapes. Reach her at ashar@hbr.net or lashar@wickenslaw.com.

Index

#

A

B

C

D

E

F

G

H

I

J

K

L

M

N

O

P